PARDONED TO BE
PRIESTS

PARDONED TO BE PRIESTS

Living life the way God intended

J. GERALD HARRIS

C. Barry McCarty

TMU
PRESS
Truett McConnell
University

Truett McConnell University

Dedication

I would like to dedicate this book to my great-grandson, *William James Echols*. By the time this book is published he will only be one year old, but he has brought incredible joy into our lives. His birth reminded us that we have a God who is a miracle worker. He is a happy little boy who has great spiritual potential. I do not know what kind of world he will encounter as he grows and matures, but his parents Taylor and Hayley and our entire family will nurture him in the Lord. We are confident our God, who is able, will call him into His family, grant him incredible gifts and use him to have an impact upon our world for the glory of His Great Name.

Contents

Foreword

Human beings were made to love and be loved by God—not as a distant, impersonal deity who created the world and to whom we occasionally say thanks for a warm planet with blue oceans and gardens with ripe tomatoes, but as a loving heavenly Father who knows us better than our closest friend or next of kin, and whose tender affection toward us is best described by a beautiful word that Miles Coverdale coined for his 1535 English translation of the Bible: *lovingkindness*. It was that kind of relationship with God that moved King David to exclaim: "You make known to me the path of life; in your presence there is fullness of joy; at your right hand are pleasures forevermore."[i]

Sadly, that intimate fellowship with God for which we were created and that our first parents Adam and Eve enjoyed in the Garden of Eden before the Fall was broken by their sin and rebellion. And they passed on to the human race a broken nature that has perpetuated that ancient sinful rebellion in every generation since. Thus the story of the Bible is the story of God's redeeming us from our loss of fellowship with him in paradise. To that end, the early chapters of the Bible tell of God's calling first a man, then a family, and then a nation into a personal, covenant relationship with himself. When Abraham began to worship and call upon the Lord, the Lord promised to make him a great nation, to give him a land, and to bless all of the nations of the earth through his people who would live in that Promised Land. From that one man God created a family—Abraham, Isaac, and Jacob. From that family—from the sons of Jacob—came the twelve tribes of Israel. From those twelve tribes God created the nation of Israel under the Law of Moses, a Constitution written on tablets of stone by God's own hand. And fourteen centuries later, from that nation came a man like no other. A man who was one person with two natures: the human nature of a Jewish descendant of Abraham and the divine nature of the only-begotten Son of God, Jesus Christ. That is the story of the Bible, the story of our redemption, and at its core it is all about God's desire to make his people fit to live in his holy presence forever.

It took thousands of years for God to prepare the way to draw his people near to himself again. When the people of Israel set up the tabernacle, God made his presence known to them by means of a spectacular glowing cloud that filled the most holy part of the building and also rested above it. Even in the middle of the night, the Shekinah cloud could still be seen as a pillar of fire hovering over the Tabernacle. No matter what time of day you looked toward the center of the Israelite camp, there it was—and there He was! When the temple in Jerusalem replaced the tabernacle as Israel's permanent house of worship, God filled that building, too, with the cloud of his glory. But the Mosaic laws and rituals of the Old Testament could only foreshadow the mysteries that the New Testament would fulfill with the coming of Jesus Christ as our great high priest, who by means of a better sacrifice opened for us a better way into a better sanctuary. For fourteen hundred years the veil of the Temple hung with its solemn injunction not to draw near. Then for thirty-three years the Son of God himself—his human ancestry not of the priestly tribe of Levi but of the royal tribe of Judah—had to live on the outside of that veil. But with his death, resurrection, and ascension into heaven, all of that changed forever as he opened for us the way into the eternal, heavenly sanctuary of God's presence.

The great work of Christ is to bring us near to the Father, to bring us inside the veil. In the earthly sanctuary of the Old Testament, only one man, the high priest, was allowed to pass through the veil into the presence of God, and he but once a year on the Day of Atonement. So the fulfillment of those shadowy mysteries—the atoning death of Christ on the cross, the shedding of his blood as our cleansing sacrifice, his bodily resurrection from the grave, and his glorious ascension into the heavenly sanctuary—these all have this end: that believers who are cleansed of their sins by the blood of Christ are brought near to live in God's presence forever. The work that Christ has *done for us* brings us to God so that he may *do in us* the greater work of making us his royal priesthood.

"Therefore, brothers," says the writer of Hebrews, "since we have confidence to enter the holy places by the blood of Jesus, by the new and living way that he opened for us through the curtain, that is, through his flesh, and since we have a great priest over the house of God, let us draw near."[ii] Those who once could not pass inside the veil, God now invites to draw near. Thus the priesthood of all believers is one of the great doctrines of the Bible.

The priesthood of all believers is also one of the great biblical doctrines recovered by the Protestant Reformation. Breaking with the beliefs of the medieval Roman church, the Reformers held that there is no longer an exclusive priestly class within God's people, but, by virtue of our union with Christ, all believers share in Christ's priestly status. Jesus Christ, the great high priest, is the final mediator between God and his people, a role that we share with and through him. The doctrine of the priesthood of all believers broke the hold of the Roman church on the people, who were no longer forced to depend upon a priestly class to read and interpret the Bible for them, confer the forgiveness of sins through rites and rituals, or mediate any other of God's gifts and graces. While recognizing the place that God gave pastors and deacons to provide sound teaching and leadership in the church, those roles are exercised in light of the fact that the ground at the foot of the Cross is level, and all believers—ordained ministers and church members alike—are equally priests through Christ. Among the descendants of the Reformation, Baptists have held this doctrinal distinction especially dear.

Given the biblical and historical importance of the doctrine, it made sense that in 1988 a Baptist pastor, J. Gerald Harris, would preach and later publish a series of sermons on the subject—the first edition of the present volume that you now hold in your hands. The priesthood of the believer is one of those key biblical themes that bears repeating in every generation. But the immediate catalyst for Harris' *Pardoned to Be Priests* also reveals a third reason that the doctrine has been prominent in Christian history. At times, liberal theologians have misused the priestly principle that every believer has the right to interpret the Bible for himself to undermine strong biblical preaching and pastoral leadership. Worse yet, they have twisted it to undermine the historic, orthodox understanding of the inspiration, inerrancy, and authority of Scripture, or to water-down other biblical doctrines that liberals view as outdated for more progressive times.

In the 1980s the struggle between orthodoxy and theological modernism saw the rise of the Conservative Resurgence in the Southern Baptist Convention as Baptists sought to reclaim their seminaries, publishing house, and other institutions that had drifted to the left theologically. In 1987, the Convention Press created a firestorm with the release of a doctrinal study by Walter B. Shurden on *The Doctrine of the Priesthood of the Believer.*[iii] Shurden was Dean of the School of Theology at Southern Seminary in Louisville before joining the theology faculty at Mercer University, and one of the prominent Baptist academics who viewed the conservative movement not as a resurgence, but as a "Fundamentalist Takeover" of their convention.

Many of the leaders of the Conservative Resurgence were strong preachers who filled prominent pulpits in Baptist life: men like Adrian Rogers at Bellevue Baptist Church in Memphis, Jimmy Draper at First Baptist Euless, Charles Stanley at First Baptist Atlanta, Jerry Vines at First Baptist Jacksonville, and the venerable W. A. Criswell at First Baptist Dallas. These men spoke with great power and authority because they believed unreservedly in the power and authority of Scripture; they believed that God had spoken clearly, sufficiently, and without error in the Bible. Shurden's book was, in part, a thinly veiled attack on the strong voices of these conservative leaders for biblical authority. Most readers knew who the enemy was when Shurden declared that laypeople needed "a shield from theological tyranny and authoritarianism."[iv] When he took the priesthood of believers in hand as a whip to drive out pastors who were "monopolistic managers of the church, authoritative interpreters of Scripture, and sole mediators between God and human souls," he didn't have progressive theologians at a seminary wine and cheese party in mind.[v] Those attacks were aimed at men like Criswell, who expressed himself in such books as *Why I Preach That the Bible Is Literally True*.

The priesthood of the believer became a wedge issue for moderates and liberals who accused conservatives of elevating pastors to positions of authority in the churches they served and in convention life. And conservatives pushed back on liberals' misuse of the doctrine. In 1988 I was on the platform with SBC President Adrian Rogers in San Antonio, serving as his chief parliamentarian, when the resolutions committee presented and the messengers adopted a resolution critical of the liberal interpretation of the priesthood of the believer and soul competency. The view that prevailed when messengers from the churches spoke to the issue is reflected well by our author here in this volume:

> The believer-priest, illuminated by the Holy Spirit, has the right to interpret the Scripture for himself. He does not have the right to add anything or subtract anything from the Word of God.[vi]

Shurden's book also addressed one of the other hotly contested issues during the Resurgence: the ordination of women.

> Just as the doctrine of the priesthood of believers universalized the priesthood in terms of race and sex, it also universalized the priesthood in terms of vocation of calling and location of calling. . . .
>
> . . . No longer is the priesthood restricted to males from the tribe of Levi. The unmistakable teaching of the New Tes-

tament is that the old class priesthood of Judaism has been transformed into the universal priesthood of all Christians. [vii]

Just before the release of Shurden's book, Gerald Harris, then pastor of Colonial Heights Baptist Church in Jackson, Mississippi, was serving on the Southern Baptist Sunday School Board and saw an advanced copy. Concerned with what the Convention Press was offering as a doctrinal study from a Baptist scholar, Harris decided that Baptist people in the pews needed a counterbalance to Shurden's views. What was initially preached as a series of sermons for his congregation was, at the urging of conservative friends, soon published by Broadman Press under the title: *Pardoned to Be Priests*. Even apart from the historical circumstances that birthed it, this book is a good study of the biblical doctrine of the priesthood of all believers. But seen in the light of those times, it stands as a specific example of the kinds of errors that faithful Baptist preachers were trying to correct within their own denominational family during the Battle for the Bible. As our author puts it:

> Some contend that historically Baptists have held to the concept of soul competency or soul liberty, allowing that God has given to every person the right to interpret the Scriptures for himself. One must remember, however, that liberty is not license, and soul liberty historically was never understood to mean that one could freely believe contrary to his church's doctrinal statement and still be its salaried servant. [viii]

That W.A. Criswell wrote the foreword for the first edition of *Pardoned to Be Priests* speaks to the significance of this issue in Baptist history and the importance of the church's getting this doctrine right in every generation.

I have known Gerald Harris since those early years of the Conservative Resurgence—including his 15-year tenure as the editor of the *Christian Index*, the nation's oldest continuously published Christian newspaper—and I have found him to be a biblically faithful preacher and an honest journalist who, while conservative in his editorial opinions, nevertheless always sought to be fair and accurate in his work as a journalist. I am pleased to commend the updated edition of *Pardoned to be Priests: Living life the way God intended* to pastors who are preparing to preach on the subject, to Bible study leaders looking for a good lesson guide, or to any believer who yearns to better understand the exalted position that God has called us to as part of his royal priesthood.

The redemptive work of the Father and the Son *for us* find their completion in the work of the Holy Spirit *within us*, transforming us into holy priests who enjoy eternal access to God's glorious presence. To this we are called and for this the mighty power of God is working in the heart of every believer. One of the most fervent prayers to flow from the lips of King David expresses this preeminent cry of his heart: "One thing have I asked of the Lord, that will I seek after: that I may dwell in the house of the Lord all the days of my life, to gaze upon the beauty of the Lord and to inquire in his temple."[ix] The priesthood of the believer is our way through the veil of the heavenly sanctuary into the intimate, innermost presence of God, both now and for eternity.

Read on, dear friend, and draw near!

C. Barry McCarty, PhD
Professor of Rhetoric and Communication
Truett McConnell University
Cleveland, GA

[i] Psalm 16:11.

[ii] Hebrews 10:19-22.

[iii] Walter B. Shurden, *The Doctrine of the Priesthood of Believers* (Convention Press, 1987).

[iv] Shurden, p. 137

[v] Shurden, p. 134.

[vi] See p. xxx

[vii] Shurden, pp. 122, 138.

[viii] See p. xxx.

[ix] Psalm 27:4

Author's Appreciation

I doubt if I have ever done anything without a significant amount of help from others. In the revision of this volume, *Pardoned to be Priests: Living life the way God intended*, I have had people that have greatly assisted me in the process. First, I want to express my gratitude to Dr. Barry McCarty, who wrote the Foreword. Dr. McCarty has become the personification of wisdom and grace to Southern Baptists as the parliamentarian of our Convention. He is also an extraordinary scholar and professor with great expertise in the area of rhetoric and homiletics. Furthermore, he is a warm-hearted Christian gentleman and treasured friend.

Peter Lumpkins is likewise worthy of recognition and appreciation because of his role as the Director of TMU Press at Truett McConnell University. He maintains a busy schedule not only as director of publishing but also as Associate Professor of History and Christian Studies at the university. He provided counsel, guidance, leadership and editing without which this book would have never been published. He is also a dear friend and partnering with him on any project is a supernal joy.

Most of all, I want to thank my wife, Martha Jean, who rejoiced when I announced my retirement a couple of years ago, but who has seen little evidence of me being put out to pasture. I have disappeared to my study every morning and most afternoons to work on sermons, on this book or other writing assignments dear to my heart. Her extreme patience, unconditional love and unwavering support have been an untold blessing during this season of our lives. I have read the revised portions of the book to her, including the section in which I declare my strong views on complementarianism and have received her blessings and agreement. She is the best!

Preface

The present volume, *Pardoned to be Priests: Living life the way God intended*, explores the vital Christian principle of the priesthood of the believer. The core beliefs presented here were first published in 1988 by Broadman Press, and the foreword was written by one of my heroes, Dr. W. A. Criswell, who then was near the end of his fifty-year ministry as pastor of First Baptist Church in Dallas, Texas.

The occasion for publishing the first edition was the 1988 annual doctrinal study for Southern Baptists, a convention-wide study focusing on the priesthood of the believer. However, the position in the book published for Southern Baptists to study the believer's priesthood revealed a decidedly liberal slant.

Consequently, I preached a series of sermons at my church examining the believer's priesthood both biblically and historically the way Baptists had widely understood it. The sermons were later revised for publication at the suggestion of several friends. The Baptist Sunday School Board's publishing house (now LifeWay Christian Resources) was gracious enough to put the messages into print.

Many years have lapsed since 1988. But I believe these messages are more needed now than ever. The priesthood of the believer remains a biblical doctrine that must be preached, taught, instilled, and applied in every Christian's life no matter his or her denominational background. Thus, a deep conviction about the spiritual significance of this doctrine inevitably led me to work toward an update to the 1988 edition.

As I proceeded to update the first edition, TMU Press, the academic publishing arm of Truett McConnell University in Cleveland, Georgia took a publishing interest in the new manuscript. Indeed the interest TMU Press displayed confirmed in my heart the Holy Spirit's leading in pursuing this fresh edition of the believer's priesthood.

Furthermore, as I was both thrilled and humbled that Dr. Criswell penned the Foreword to the first edition, another of my heroes of the faith, Dr. Barry McCarty, Professor of Rhetoric and Communication at Truett McConnell University graciously desired to pen the Foreword to the present edition.

In the midst of the COVID-19 Coronavirus of 2020 many people were in a panic and looking for hope and help. The virus started in China, but it was not long until the United States was the nation most dramatically impacted by the dreadful pandemic. Almost every nation on earth felt this dreaded scourge. Most Americans watched with horror as news reports gave the escalating numbers of those who had contracted the virus and those who had died. Government restrictions were mandated that altered life in America drastically. Other countries imposed similar limitations.

In the midst of the crisis Pope Francis made a statement on March 20 during his live-streaming morning Mass that arrested my attention. He said, "People who cannot get to confession because of the coronavirus lock-down or another serious reasons can go to God directly, be specific about their sins, request pardon and experience God's loving forgiveness."

Going directly to God has been a hallmark of Christians since the veil in the temple was rent in twain at the time of Christ's crucifixion. It is good that the Roman Catholic church is finally catching up with this cherished Christian principle. You don't have to go to the Catholic church to find a priest. Every believer is a priest. The Apostle Peter wrote to believers and stated, "But you are a chosen people, a royal priesthood, a holy nation, His own special people, that you may proclaim the praises of Him who called you out of darkness into His marvelous light" (1 Pt 2:9, NKJV).

Many believers are living beneath their privileges because they do not realize the riches of their inheritance in Christ Jesus. Hopefully, this book will help you discover what it means to be a New Testament priest with all the privileges, access, rights and joys of those who are a part of God's royal priesthood.

J. Gerald Harris

Spring, 2021

I

I

❦

The Consecration of Priests
(Leviticus 8:1-36)

To understand fully what the Bible says about the priest-
hood of the believer, one must begin the study in the Old
Testament. The Pentateuch contains a wealth of information about the
Levitical priesthood. Comprehending this priesthood as typified by
Aaron and his sons is foundational and essential to an understanding of
the doctrine of the priesthood of the believer.

Aaron, the first high priest, is a symbol or a type of the Lord Jesus
Christ, our Great High Priest. The sons of Aaron serve as representa-
tives of the believer-priests who constitute the New Testament church.
Initially, it will be helpful to consider some of the parallels between Old
Testament priests and present-day priests, for believers in the Lord Je-
sus Christ are "a royal priesthood" (1 Pt 2:9) and "a kingdom of priests"
(Rv 5:10, GNT).

In the eighth chapter of Leviticus, Aaron and his sons, the first
priests in Israel, were inducted into their office by a solemn service
of consecration. God's instructions to Moses about the consecration of
priests (Ex 28—29) were carried out by Moses (Lv 8). There is much in

this Old Testament ceremony of consecration that is applicable for believer-priests today.

I. THE CHOOSING OF AARON AND HIS SONS

God in His grace and wisdom chose Aaron and his sons to be priests in Israel. God said to Moses: "Now take Aaron your brother, and his sons with him, from among the children of Israel, that he may minister to Me as priest, Aaron and Aaron's, sons: Nadab, Abihu, Eleazar, and Ithamar. (Ex 28:1). In a similar fashion the Lord Jesus Christ has chosen us in Him to constitute a spiritual priesthood. Before Jesus went to the cross, He declared to His disciples: "You did not choose Me, but I chose you and appointed you that you should go and bear fruit," (Jn 15:16a). The idea is that we are chosen for salvation and ordained for service. We are not saved to sit in flowery meadows, making daisy chains while the world disintegrates. We are saved to go, to minister, to "bring forth fruit." We must forever remember that we are not only a sampling of the saved but also a company of priests with solemn responsibilities.

Wherever churches are able to instill in their members that they are ministers and priests, they provide a proving ground upon which God can move in mighty power. It would be glorious beyond measure if every believer were to give of himself in unflinching, sacrificial service to the kingdom of God. Paul made reference to this priestly office when he declared: "I beseech you therefore, brethren, by the mercies of God that ye present your bodies a living sacrifice, holy, acceptable unto God, which is your reasonable service" (Rm 12:1).

A study of the priesthood of the Old Testament and the priesthood of the New Testament will immediately reveal a fundamental difference. "In the Old Testament the priest offered the sacrifice. In the New Testament the priest is the sacrifice. He offers his life to God on behalf of the world which God is seeking to redeem."[1] So, let us remember that we have been chosen for salvation and ordained for service.

Always there are individuals who remonstrate against such a noble calling, saying, "I am not very important. I am not a gifted person. I have very little ability. God would never choose me for divine service." Perhaps there is comfort in knowing that even the high priests of the Old Testament were chosen from among weak and feeble men.

Indeed, the priests had to meet certain requirements. They had to have a measure of personal maturity (Nm 4:3). They had to have a measure of sexual purity (Lv 21:16-24). Nevertheless, God had to choose His priests from among men who were much less than perfect. In fact, men from the tribe of Levi were chosen to serve as priests. The tribe of Levi was undoubtedly one of the least respected, least honored of all of the tribes. Levi, the fountainhead of the tribe, killed a man (Gn 49:5-7). Consequently, his descendants lived under a curse. Yet God took imperfect men from this ignominious tribe and set them up to serve as priests in Israel. The Bible says: "For the law appoints as high priests men who have weakness, but the word of the oath, which came after the law, *appoints* the Son who has been perfected forever" (Heb 7:28).

There is a consecration and a perpetuity about the priesthood of Christ that is unrivaled. But the Scripture also affirms that God will choose men for service who have infirmities. What an encouragement that ought to be to the modern-day believer!

We know from the Scriptures that God chose people with little ability. He chose Moses, who objected vehemently, "O my Lord, I *am* not eloquent, neither before nor since You have spoken to Your servant; but I *am* slow of speech and [a]slow of tongue" (Ex 4:10). He chose Gideon, who argued, "O my Lord, how can I save Israel? Indeed, my clan *is* the weakest in Manasseh, and I *am* the least in my father's house." (Jgs 6:15). He chose Jeremiah, who protested, "Ah, Lord God! behold, I cannot speak for I am a youth" (Jer 1:6). He chose Amos, who declared that he was neither a prophet nor the son of a prophet (Am 7:14). When Jesus chose His disciples, He ended up with a ragtag and dubious cadre of outcasts that included peasants, fishermen, a guerilla fighter and even a despised publican.

Not only does God often choose people with little ability, but He also chooses people with few resources. He chose Shamgar, whose only weapon against the Philistines was an ox goad. He chose Samson, whose total arsenal against the enemy consisted of the jawbone of an ass. He sent David up against the giant Goliath with his hotshot slingshot and a few pebbles. He chose a little lad with his modest lunch as the one through whom the Lord fed the thousands.

The greatest danger in the church is not that there will be a shortage of ability or a limited number of physical resources. In fact, the wealth of the church could be her most formidable arrearage and her ability her greatest liability. There is always the danger of becoming like the Laodiceans who boasted, "(We are) rich, have become wealthy, and have need of nothing" (Rv 3:17).

Does your church have a multitude of millionaires? A row of Rhodes scholars? A collection of college presidents? An army of all-American football players? A majority of multitalented people? If the answer is yes, your church might be in serious trouble.

The church that is constituted with a host of nobodies could be in terrific shape and, thus, a prime candidate for God to use in His service. The Bible says: "For you see your calling, brethren, that not many wise according to the flesh, not many mighty, not many noble, *are called.* But God has chosen the foolish things of the world to put to shame the wise, and God has chosen the weak things of the world to put to shame the things which are mighty; and the base things of the world and the things which are despised God has chosen, and the things which are not, to bring to nothing the things that are, that no flesh should glory in His presence" (1 Cor 1:26-29).

The believer has been chosen, ordained, appointed and set apart for the purpose of rendering priestly service to God. It will be a good day, a great day, a glory hallelujah day, when every child of God, every re-deemed soul and every born-again saint of God understands that truth. Just think of what would happen if every child of God determined to minister in the marketplace as a servant of the Lord Jesus Christ!

A number of years ago I was in Anaheim Stadium on the Fourth of July to see a baseball game between the California Angels and the Boston Red Sox. There were 35,000 to 40,000 people in the stadium that night. During the seventh inning stretch, everyone in the stadium was given a candle. The stadium lights were extinguished, and the candles were lit. We stood with our lighted candles to show our solidarity, our unity, our common support for the land that we love. An enormous cheer burst forth from the stadium as the darkness was overcome by the lighted candles of the thousands who proudly held up their symbols of unity. Today in stadiums all across America tens of thousands of sports fans are often directed to turn on their smartphone flashlights to illuminate the darkness and the spectacle it creates always elicits an uproarious response.

We may be assured that a great cheer would burst forth from the throne room of heaven if the inhabitants of glory could ever see vast multitudes of God's saints letting their lights shine on earth in compassionate service and in bold witness.

II. THE CLEANSING OF AARON AND HIS SONS

Having chosen Aaron and his sons to serve as priests, God commanded Moses to gather the people together for a solemn convocation. Jehovah God wanted the people to witness the ordination ceremony. The first part of the ceremony involved the cleansing of Aaron and his sons. The Bible says, "Then Moses brought Aaron and his sons, and washed them with water" (Lv 8:6). The basic idea conveyed by this ceremonial washing is that those who render service toward God must be clean and pure.

Actually, the word "wash" (rah-ghatz) in Leviticus 8:6 is a general term and lends itself to two different interpretations. It can signify the washing of the whole body in water. It can also refer to what is commonly called a birdbath, where only the hands or face is washed.

In the New Testament there are two very distinct words to differentiate between the two types of bathing. The word "louo" refers to a complete washing of the whole body. That means to get into the bathtub or shower and scrub sparkling clean with bath soap. The word "nipto" refers to a partial washing of the hands or the feet.

For example, in John 13, we have the record of Jesus washing the feet of the disciples. Peter protested, saying, "You shall never wash my feet" (v. 8). After a brief conversation to capture Peter's obedience, Jesus said, "He that is washed [*louo*] needeth not save to wash [*nipto*] his feet but is clean every whit" (v. 10, KJV). What Jesus was saying is this: He who has the initial washing of regeneration needs only to have a continual cleansing to remove the daily defilement of sin.

So, the believer-priest has been cleansed by the blood of the Lamb once and for all. The apostle Paul declared, "Not by works or righteousness which we have done, but according to his mercy he saved us, by the washing of regeneration and renewing of the Holy Ghost" (Ti 3:5, KJV).

In addition to the judicial washing of the blood, there is the daily washing of the Word of God. The Psalmist asked a colossal and universal question, "How can a young man cleanse his way?" Then under the inspiration of the Holy Spirit, he proposed the answer, "by taking heed according to My word" (Ps 119:9).

This principle is reinforced by the high priestly prayer of Jesus, who said, "Sanctify them by your truth: Your word is truth" (Jn 17:17). The cleansing agent for the defiled believer-priest is the Word of God.

Under the old covenant the priests were never permitted to touch holy things anywhere in that "tabernacle of old" until they had washed at the laver. In fact, if they touched anything that was holy with unclean hands, they were smitten with death.

All too often we rush in where angels fear to tread. We stumble through our Sunday School lessons, our choir rehearsals, our committee meetings, and wonder why there is a deadness and a lifelessness to our activities. We come to worship and go away unmoved, unbroken, and unprepared to face another week. The problem? Attempting to minister, attempting to serve, attempting to touch holy things with unwashed hands! The whole day, from the beginning of the morning to the setting of the sun, may pass without many Christians having had one moment of quiet time in the cleansing, purifying Word of God.

It is ironic that our preparation for worship each Sunday includes the washing of our bodies, the manicuring of our nails, the styling of our hair and dressing appropriately for the occasion, but there is little or no little heart preparation. There is no application of the water of the Word to cleanse and refresh the soul. It would be better to rush into the Oval Office of the White House in filthy rags to render service to the President of the United States than to propose to serve the Lord with a defiled and unclean spirit.

III. THE CLOTHING OF AARON AND HIS SONS

Leviticus 8:7-9 lists the apparel of Aaron, the high priest of Israel. You will note that he was attired with seven articles of clothing. These articles symbolized the lofty and noble office of high priest. Three of the articles were worn exclusively by him. Four of the articles were common to all of the priests. We shall give our attention to these four articles of clothing, common to all priests. Three of these articles of apparel are mentioned in verse 13: "Then Moses brought Aaron's sons and put tunics on them, girded them with sashes, and put [a]hats on them, as the Lord had commanded Moses" (Lv 8:13).

1. Coats: Righteousness

The coats which represent spotless righteousness are mentioned first. We find this same word in Genesis 3:21: "Also for Adam and his wife the Lord God made tunics of skin, and clothed them". The Lord made a provision whereby Adam and Eve could be acceptable to a Holy God. He gave them coats because people cannot enter into the presence of God except there be a covering. Man is a sinner, and God is holy.

Just as the fig leaves did not suffice as a covering for Adam and Eve, our own righteousness will not suffice for us. Therefore, God made the provision for us in His Son. At Calvary Jesus laid aside His righteousness and took upon Himself our nakedness in order that we might be clothed in His righteousness. Paul wrote, "But put on the Lord Jesus Christ" (Rm 13:14). He also said that God has made Christ to be "unto us wisdom, and righteousness, and sanctification, and redemption" (1 Cor 1:30, KJV).

The Psalmist said, "Let Your priests be clothed with righteousness; and let Your saints shout for joy. I will also clothe her priests with salvation" (132:9,16). When we trust in Jesus, we put on the garment of righteousness and salvation.

2. Girdles: Readiness

"Girdles" are next mentioned as the apparel for the priests. This garment stands for *readiness*. In the East, people wear long, flowing garments. When there is a need for rapidity of movement, these garments are pulled up and tucked into the girdle. When it came time for the Exodus of the Israelites out of Egypt, God instructed them to eat the Passover in readiness for their journey. He said, "And thus you shall eat it, with your belt on your waist, your sandals on your feet, and your staff in your hand. So, you shall eat it in haste" (Ex 12:11).

In Lk 12:35-36, the Lord challenged His disciples to be ready for His return: "Let your waist be girded and your lamps burning; and yourselves be like men who wait for their master." When the church prayed for Peter's deliverance from prison, the liberating angel came to the rescue and ordered a hasty escape. The angel said to Peter, "Gird yourself and tie on your sandals. . . .. Put on your garment and follow me" (Ac 12:8).

A little boy rushed into his house after Sunday School one Lord's Day. He said, "Momma, my Sunday School teacher told our class that this world is only a place in which God lets us live so that we may get ready for the world to come. Why is it I don't see anybody getting ready?"

This article of clothing worn by the Levitical priests suggests that we as believer-priests are to be ready always. We are to be constantly working, witnessing, and watching for the Lord's return.

3. Bonnets: Reverence

The third article of apparel mentioned in our text is the "bonnets."

They represent *reverence.* Orthodox Jews traditionally keep their heads covered when entering their temples of worship. Even when reading the Bible privately, they give meticulous care to the covering of their heads. For centuries anyone approaching the Wailing Wall in Jerusalem was required by the Jews to have his head covered. It is a sign of reverence.

It is also a recognition of the superiority of Christ. As believer-priests we have been elevated to a high position. In fact, Paul in Ephesians declared that even now we are privileged to sit with Christ in heavenly places. Nevertheless, a believer-priest is to remain continually in subjection to the revealed will of God.

4. Trousers: Renunciation

The final article of clothing for the priests of the Old Testament was "trousers." That garment is not mentioned in Leviticus 8 but is included in the priest's attire in Exodus 28:42: "And you shall make for them linen trousers to cover their nakedness; they shall reach from the waist to the thighs." This garment speaks of *renunciation.* If the priest is to function in the power of the living God, he must renounce the self-life.

Unfortunately, in our churches it appears that there is too much of "self" on parade. It has been said, "That which is of the flesh is bad anywhere, but it is most of all out of place in the holy service of God."[2] The Bible says, "So then, those who are in the flesh cannot please God" (Rm 8:8).

As long as we try to operate in the flesh, we just spin our wheels; but when we learn to depend on God and operate in the Spirit, things begin to happen. Before Jonathan Edwards preached his sermon, "Sinners, in the Hands of an Angry God," he, according to history, renounced his flesh. He refused to eat for three days. He refused to sleep for three nights. He prayed; he yielded himself to God; he believed. The impact of that sermon is still felt in America today.

The "trousers" worn by the priests signify to us as believer-priests that the flesh must be renounced and that we must yield ourselves to the Holy Spirit. He is our strength. He is our power.

IV. THE CONSECRATION OF AARON AND HIS SONS

The ordination ceremony was highlighted by the anointing of Aaron and the sacrificial service. First, Moses took the anointing oil and anointed the tabernacle, the altar, and the sacred vessels in the tabernacle. Then the Scripture says, "And he poured some of the anointing oil upon Aaron's head, and anointed him, to consecrate him" (Lv 8:12). This foreshadows the anointing of Jesus, our Great High Priest, who was the anointed one from His birth, but who was anointed for His ministry at the time of His baptism. This seems to be confirmed by the statement of Jesus in Lk 4:18: "The Spirit of the Lord is upon me, because He has anointed me..."

There is a reference to the anointing of Aaron's sons in Leviticus 8:30: "Then Moses took some of the anointing oil and some of the blood that was upon the altar, and sprinkled it upon Aaron, on his garments, on his sons, and on the garments of his sons with him; and he consecrated Aaron, his garments, his sons, and the garments of his sons with him." Today believer-priests receive the anointing of the Holy Spirit by virtue of their union with the risen Christ, the Great High Priest.

The psalmist declared, "Behold, how good and how pleasant it is for brethren to dwell together in unity! It is like the precious oil upon the head, running down on the beard, the beard of Aaron, running down on the edge of his garments" (133:1-2). The anointing oil flowed down the skirts of Aaron's garments. This anointing is highly significant because Aaron's garments portray him as one who stood before God on behalf of others. It speaks of the partnership between his anointing oil and all those whom he represented before God.

As believers we, too, have received an anointing for ministry from Christ, the anointed One. Preachers occasionally speak of "an anointing from God" or "divine unction" or "an enduement of power"; such phrases have, for the most part, become glib clichés and meaningless theological jargon. In this day most of what happens in churches can be explained in human terms. Church programs are carried out with Madison Avenue promotional gimmicks, and organizational structures are produced by computerized wizardry. Marketing techniques have developed seeker-sensitive, consumer-friendly, non-threatening approaches to drawing a crowd of people, but we must remember that a crowd doesn't necessarily translate into a consecrated fellowship of Christians.

On Mount Carmel, Elijah didn't have to hire a child prodigy to play a saxophone to get his point across. John the Baptist didn't have to promise that he would appear before his followers as a three-dimensional image formed by the interference of light beams from a mysterious coherent laser to ensure a successful spiritual experience. At Pentecost Peter didn't have to create Hollywood-quality videos in order to keep up the interest, but three thousand souls were saved.

Genuine revival requires more than glitter and gimmicks and special guests. A soul-stirring revival requires the power of God, the anointing of God. Where there is no anointing, preaching and ministry avail little. It is like rowing a boat with a toothpick, like driving a nail with a feather, like trying to hit a baseball with a cotton string, like going on a lion hunt with a flyswatter. But Aaron was anointed, set apart, sanctified for special service. In the final analysis the anointing of God is a special touch for a specific task.

1. The Sin Offering

After the anointing of Aaron, the sacrificial service began with a series of offerings. The first offering brought by Moses was "the bull for the sin offering" (Lv 8:14). Aaron and his sons placed their hands upon the head of the bullock. In this act they typically transferred their sins from themselves upon the sacrificial animal. In doing so, they experienced the forgiveness of God for sin. Those who serve the Lord in ministry must first be reconciled to God through the forgiveness of sin.

2. The Burnt Offering

The second offering mentioned is "the burnt offering" (Lv 8:18).

Moses brought a ram for this offering. Once again, Aaron and his son placed their hands upon the victim to be sacrificed. Moses killed the animal and "burned the whole ram on the altar" (v. 21). The fact that the sacrifice was totally consumed has given rise to the term "whole burnt offering." This offering speaks of a true yieldedness and allegiance to the Lord. The minister must not only be reconciled to God but also must be prepared to give of himself totally and sacrificially to God (note Rm 12:1).

3. The Offering of Consecration

The third offering of great significance mentioned in the sacrificial service is "the ram of consecration" (Lv 8:22). Aaron and his sons were instructed to lay their hands upon this ram. The sacrifice was slain. Its blood was applied to the tip of the right ear, to the right thumb, and to the right big toe of each priest. To them it meant their ears were to hear the Word of God, their hands were to do the work of God, and their feet were to carry them in the way of God.

Generally, blood is a cleansing agent in the Scripture, but here it signifies purpose. The blood on the priest's ear signifies the use intended for the ear. We are to keep our ears tuned to the Word of God. But all too often we are dull of hearing (Heb 5:11). We listen to the wrong voices (Ps 1:1).

When Eve was looking at the fruit of the forbidden tree, she listened to the wrong voice. The serpent contradicted God when he said to Eve, "You will not surely die; For God knows that in the day you eat of it then your eyes will be opened, and you will be like God, knowing good and evil" (Gn 3:4,5).

The children of Israel listened to the wrong voices when they accepted the report of the ten spies and rejected the report of the two spies (Caleb and Joshua). Because they rebelled against the God-honored report, they were divinely sentenced to forty years of wandering in the wilderness.

Job was greatly afflicted and, in the course of time, bombarded with many voices. For example, there was the counsel of his wife who said, "curse God and die!" (Jb 2:9).

Elijah was a man who diligently sought to hear from God. He went to stand upon the mountain before the Lord. A mighty wind came and tore the mountains asunder. An earthquake shook the very ground where Elijah stood. A fire came to scorch the earth. Elijah looked and listened, but the Lord was not in the wind, the earthquake, or the fire. But after all the calamity and clamor, Elijah heard God in a still, small voice.

The great desire of the believer-priest must be the desire of the psalmist who said, "I will hear what God the Lord will speak" (85:8). Jesus said, "Therefore whosoever hears these sayings of Mine, and does them, I will liken him unto a wise man. . ." (Mt 7:24).

With spiritual ears believers need to hear the still, small voice of the Spirit. Too many are listening to well-meaning friends. Others are tuned in to their own reasoning. Too few are attuned to the Spirit of God. Let it be known that the Spirit speaks through the Scriptures and by this means instructs us in the will of God. Consequently, a thumbprint on the Bible is more important than a footprint on the moon. We must use our spiritual ears as God intended. We must sit daily at His feet with the Word and hear Him speak to our soul. Such a personal devotional life will motivate godly living and enhance spiritual growth.

The thumb of the right hand was also touched with the blood of the sacrifice. The blood was placed upon the thumb in order to consecrate every work performed by the priest. This small appendage is so vital to working with the hands. Grasping an object without the thumb is nearly impossible. The Levitical priests had many menial tasks to perform which required the use of their hands. They chopped wood, drew water, washed the sacred vessels in the tabernacle, and prepared the altar for use. Thus, it is significant that their hands were consecrated for the work God called them to do.

Today we know that every redeemed child of God is a priest unto God. There is the blood of consecration upon his thumb so that every menial task done in Jesus' name is consecrated by Him. The most unpleasant task performed by the preschool teacher, the most strenuous task performed by the church custodian, the most thankless task performed by the godly mother who works with her hands to provide a Christian surrounding for her children, God desires to bless and consecrate.

Consider also the spiritual Sunday School teacher, the dedicated deacon, the effective musician, and the warmhearted usher. These, and others, are the backbone of the church. Paul said, "For we are His workmanship, created in Christ Jesus for good works" (Eph 2:10). Jesus said that even a cup of cold water given in His name would not go unrewarded.

Finally, the blood of the sacrifice was placed upon the big toe of the right foot of the priest. The feet refer to the walk, or the conduct, of the believer-priest. The psalmist declared: "The steps of a good man are ordered by the Lord: and He delights in his way" (37:23). The man of God will take the steps the Lord desires him to take. Obedience is essential in the daily walk. It involves a clean separation from worldly pursuits, selections of the best instead of the good, and a clinging to the lordship of Christ.

This final sacrifice and the placing of the blood upon the ear, the thumb, and the toe, signify a consecration and a desire to know the will of God, a desire to do the work of God, and a desire to walk in the way of God. It is a total commitment to live like who we are —a royal priesthood.

We are told that during the French Revolution, the royal family in France was annihilated except for the six-year-old son of the king and queen. Many of the people called for the death of the young prince, but a more heartless suggestion was offered. They decided that they would strip the young prince of his royalty and place him in the most impoverished section of Paris to be raised by a cruel, profane woman who would doubtlessly corrupt him and raise him to be a reprobate and a disgrace to his heritage.

The woman began to try to teach the young prince to curse and swear and commit crimes of immorality. The plan backfired. Every time that evil woman tried to teach him to say a profane word or commit an immoral act, he would stomp his foot and hit his little fist on the table, and he would say, "I will not say those things and I will not do those things. I was born to be a king and I'm going to live like it!"

Dear believer, when you were redeemed by the blood of Christ, you became a child of the King. You became a saint of God. You became a royal priest. You need to live like it and walk like it.

V. THE COMMAND TO AARON AND HIS SONS

At the end of the ordination ceremony, Aaron and his sons were commanded to enter the tabernacle and remain there for seven days. The Bible says, "And you shall not go outside the door of the tabernacle of meeting for seven days, until the days of your consecration are ended. For seven days he will consecrate you" (Lv 8:33). No ministry will be powerful and impact the world profoundly that is rushed into without thought, without preparation, and without introspection.

When Paul was converted and commissioned to preach, he avowed, "I did not immediately confer with flesh and blood, nor did I go up to Jerusalem to those who were apostles before me; but I went into Arabia" (Gal 1:16-17). Paul went into the solitude of the desert so that he could be equipped and empowered for service.

Jesus commanded His first disciples to tarry in Jerusalem until the Holy Spirit endued them with power from on high. For ten days they prayed and waited for God to fill them with the Holy Spirit. Indeed, they must have suspected the futility that would come from attempting the divine work without the divine power.

In Isaiah 30:18, the Bible declares that God is waiting for those who will wait upon Him that He may be gracious unto them. The Word specifies that "those who wait on the Lord shall renew their strength; they shall mount up with wings like eagles, they shall run, and not be weary; and they shall walk, and not faint" (Is 40:31).

So, Aaron and his sons were shut up with God for seven days. On the eighth day Moses opened the tent door of the tabernacle and the men who had been set apart for sacred service made their exit from the holy place. They were ready to begin their work. Moses said, "Today the Lord will appear to you" (Lv 9:4).

In closing, note the results of a consecrated and committed priesthood. The Bible says, "And Moses and Aaron went into the tabernacle of meeting, and came out and blessed the people. Then the glory of the Lord appeared to all the people" (Lv 9:23). This verse signifies a visible, supernatural manifestation of the presence of God. When believer-priests understand who they are, the significance of their separation, the scope of their service, and the source of their strength, "the glory of the Lord [will appear] to all the people" (Lv 9:23).

Notes

1. Findley B. Edge, *The Greening of the Church* (Waco: Word Books, 1971), p. 42.
2. C. A. Coates, quoted by Arthur W. Pink, *Gleanings in Exodus* (Chicago: Moody Press, 1977), p. 277.

2

The Sin of Nadab and Abihu (Leviticus 10:1-7)

Aaron and his sons submitted to the divinely appointed procedure for induction into the priests' office (Lv 8:36). After the service of consecration, Aaron, the high priest, initiated his ministry in a most solemn and sacred manner. After he completed the administration of his first offerings as high priest, the Bible states, "Then the glory of the LORD appeared to all the people, and fire came out from before the LORD, and consumed the burnt offering and the fat on the altar. When all the people saw it, they shouted and fell on their faces" (Lv 9:23-24). This fire signified a divine approval and acceptance of the sacrificial service conducted by Aaron and his sons. The people responded to the new order of things by prostrating themselves in reverence and by shouting praise to the Lord God of Israel.

Yet how quickly the ecstasy turned into tragedy! Only the chapter divisions separate the most startling of contrasts. In Leviticus 10:1 there is the mention of a "profane fire." But by Leviticus 10:2, the confirming fire of an approving God turned into the consuming fire of an angry God.

In a moment no longer than it takes a flash of lightning to streak across the heavens, the fire of God fell upon Nadab and Abihu. While they were busily ministering in the tabernacle, God sent a fire from heaven that devoured them. Unfortunately, they had engaged in their priestly privileges without any regard for the requirements and the responsibilities incumbent upon them. Therefore, in the account of Nadab and Abihu the tragedy that comes through disobedience to the Word of God is evident. The Holy Scripture declares, "Also let the priests who come near the Lord, consecrate themselves, lest the Lord break out against them" (Ex 19:22). This chapter records the "breaking forth" of God upon a willfully disobedient and careless priesthood.

I. THE DISOBEDIENCE OF PRIESTS

God's Word declares: "Then Nadab and Abihu, the sons of Aaron, each took his censer, and put fire in it, and put incense thereon, and offered profane fire before the Lord, which He had not commanded them" (Lv 10:1). This passage plainly states that Nadab and Abihu violated a command of God. What was the nature of their violation or disobedience? There are several possibilities.

1. They Used the Wrong Fire

Each of the sons of Aaron had a "censer." This was a vessel that held coals of fire or burning embers. These newly ordained priests put fire in their censers for the purpose of igniting the wood on the altar. However, as the smoke curled up toward heaven, the Lord determined that it was from a "strange fire."

The word "profane" in Leviticus 10:1 comes from the Hebrew word "zar". It is the same word that is used to describe a false god in Psalm 81:9. It is the word used to signify an immoral woman in Proverbs 2:16. It is the word used to denote illegitimate children in Hosea 5:7. Therefore, the "profane fire" must have been taken from somewhere other than the divinely appointed place and was, therefore, unacceptable to God.

Presumably the divinely appointed place was the brazen altar. The incense fire was taken from this altar for the activities that took place on the Day of Atonement (Lv 16:12).

Concerning this altar, God told Moses, "A fire shall always be burning on the altar; it shall never go out" (Lv 6:13). There is a strong implication in the Scripture that Nadab and Abihu should have gotten the fire for their censers from the altar before the Lord, the brazen altar. Instead, they perverted God's holy plan and offered "profane fire." Because of self-confidence, Nadab and Abihu believed they could produce as good a fire as God. In the world today there are a lot of profane, strange fires. There are many imitations of that which is authentic.

Several years ago, the church I pastored rented a camp facility that was owned and operated by a religious group which held to vegetarian dietary laws. When our young people went through the cafeteria line, they discovered that the cooks had prepared various soybean recipes as a substitute for meat products. During the course of the week, there were numerous comments from the young people about having to eat fake steak and phony bologna. They were not particularly happy about having to accept a substitute for the real thing. A woman at the beach saw a number of people gathered around a man who had just been rescued from the briny sea. As she drew nearer for a closer inspection of the situation, she realized that the man receiving all of the attention was her husband. "Heavens!" she declared. "What are you doing to my husband?" The lifeguard replied, "We are giving him artificial respiration." "Artificial nothing!" she said. "Give him the real thing!"

Even as Nadab and Abihu substituted strange fire for the authentic fire of God, even so today there are multitudes who want to substitute the artificial for the authentic. There are those who want to substitute works for faith. But the Bible declares, "For by grace you have been saved through faith, and that not of yourselves; it is the gift of God, not of works, lest anyone should boast" (Eph 2:8-9). Others, perhaps unconsciously but consistently, substitute lip service for love. Paul said,

"Though I speak with the tongues of men and of angels, but have not love, I have become sounding brass or a clanging cymbal" (1 Cor 13:1).

Some get into the dilemma of substituting fighting for praying. James declared, "You fight and war. Yet you do not have because you do not ask" (Jas 4:2). And, alas, people everywhere have concocted a thousand substitutes for the power of God. Churches plan, promote, publicize, push, pull, pump, prod, and plead; yet little good is accomplished. When will believers learn that it is "not by might, nor by power, but by My Spirit, says the LORD of hosts" (Zec 4:6)?

The Spirit of God can kindle a flame of sacred love within the child of God and empower him for an effective ministry, but a strange fire, an alien fire, will curse and destroy.

Two fires became prominent in Simon Peter's life. The first was the devil's fire in the courtyard. Peter sat by that fire and denied the Lord with cursing and swearing (Mt 26:74). Less than two months later Peter got in touch with another fire. At Pentecost the Holy Spirit descended upon him as a cloven tongue of fire. This fire gave Peter the boldness to preach with a heavenly audacity that resulted in a holy harvest of souls. The right kind of fire produces divine approval, affirmation, and anointing. A strange fire results in disapproval, defeat, and death. Nadab and Abihu offered a strange fire unto the Lord. This offering may very well have been the reason they experienced divine retribution.

2. They Offered the Wrong Incense

It is also possible that Nadab and Abihu encountered the wrath of God because they used the wrong incense. God had given a very clear word of instruction concerning worship in the tabernacle. In this word of instruction was the recipe for the incense which was to be offered by the priest to God as a sweet savor of worship. Consider this recipe:

And the Lord said to Moses: "Take sweet spices, stacte and onycha and galbanum, and pure frankincense with these sweet spices; there shall be equal amounts of each. You shall make of these an incense, a compound according to the art of the perfumer, salted, pure, *and* holy. And you shall beat *some* of it very fine and put some of it before the Testimony in the tabernacle of meeting where I will meet with you. It shall be most holy to you. But *as for* the incense which you shall make, you shall not make any for yourselves, according to its composition. It shall be to you holy for the Lord. Whoever makes *any* like it, to smell it, he shall be cut off from his people." (Ex 30:34-38).

This recipe for perfume or incense was never to be employed for personal use. In fact, the death penalty was ordered by God for anyone who misused this divinely prescribed incense. This fragrance was designed by God and for God. It was undoubtedly the loveliest fragrance imaginable. When this incense rose to God's nostrils, it was a unique gift to Him.

History records that the apothecary had to cover a large geographical region in order to gather these ingredients. Once these ingredients had been gathered, they were mixed with meticulous care. The incense was thoroughly brewed and blended. Thus, it was through an expensive and complicated process that the incense was made. Like the breaking of the alabaster box and the anointing of the feet of Jesus, the offering of this incense was a demonstration of first love.

The offering of this incense is a beautiful picture of worship and adoration. Like this incense, our worship is to be a unique, separated, sanctified, holy act that ascends out of our innermost being to the very heart of God. He deserves our very best. In fact, He requests of us the first love of our hearts (Rv 2:4), the first fruit of our increase (Prv 3:9), and the first day of the week (Ac 20:7).

So often there is a reluctance to offer God the pure fragrant incense of an undivided heart. There is an unwillingness to present our bodies as a living sacrifice which is our reasonable worship (Rm 12:1). Many people worship with a halfhearted allegiance, with a time consciousness, with pride, with a devising of shortcuts, with careful calculations on how little can be given to God and yet maintain respectability.

Some church members are very much like the people an Atlanta mortician is trying to satisfy. This mortician developed a funeral home with drive-in windows to accommodate busy mourners. There are six windows where the deceased are on display. A busy mourner can drive by one of the display windows, pay his respects to the loved one or deceased friend, and be on his merry way.

That's the way many people want to worship God. They want worship to be a convenience. They want the luxury of worship without sacrifice. Such worship is in great contrast to King David who said, "Nor will I offer burnt offerings to the LORD my God with that which costs me nothing" (2 Sm 24:24).

It should also be noted here that God only accepts what He inspires. I like to think that God impresses upon my heart the sermons He wants me to preach each week. I pray, read, study, agonize, prepare my own heart, and come to the place of worship and present as an offering to God the sermon He impressed upon my heart to preach.

It should be the same way with the music. God gives the minister of music and to the choir an anthem, a song. They pray, rehearse, prepare their hearts to sing that anthem, and then they come and offer it back to God as an expression of worship.

Recently I received a call from a charming young woman who wanted to get married in our worship center. Among the songs she had chosen for her wedding was a secular love song. It so happened that I knew the song. It was a song with a soft, mellow sound and was beautifully melodious; but it would be typically sung in a ballroom or a supper club.

Believing that a wedding ceremony should be a high and holy moment of worship, I regretfully informed the prospective bride that this song would not be appropriate. Her selection of music would have been like offering the Lord incense prescribed for another. The secular song would have been a totally unacceptable offering to Him. Such music would have been like offering God meat which had been sacrificed to idols; for you see, He only accepts what He inspires.

This incense prescribed by God is especially unique because it is representative of the uniqueness of Christ. Just as no other incense would have been acceptable to God, no one can be acceptable to God except through Jesus Christ. He is the unique Son of God (Jn 3:16). He is the only way whereby we can be saved (Ac 4:12). He is the only way whereby we can have access to God (Jn 14:6). He is the one mediator between God and man (2 Tm 2:5).

God knew that men would set up their own system of priests and mediators and confessions but that a humanly devised system militates against the Word of God and violates the plan of God. The uniqueness of the incense speaks of the uniqueness of Christ. Nadab and Abihu's great error may have been the use of wrong incense.

3. They Employed the Wrong Schedule

Nadab and Abihu saw their father, Aaron, begin his priestly duties with a flourish, with the approval of God and the praise of the people. Being enamored with their new priestly positions, they decided they would launch out in their service to God. They were impulsive and impetuous.

Unfortunately, they got ahead of God. There was a prescribed time and order for all that the priests were assigned to do. A priest was to officiate at an offering each morning and each evening (Ex 30:7). Each priest was given a carefully prescribed schedule of service. Nadab and Abihu attempted to undertake their priestly duties immediately following the offerings of Aaron without regard for the schedule God had ordained.

All too often there is the impulse to rush in and do something for God when there is the need to wait upon the Lord.

An inebriated man hailed a taxi in New York City. As he climbed into the cab, he said, "Take me to Central Park and drive around the park eighteen times." As the driver was making his first circuit of the park, his drunken passenger banged on the window partition and said, "Go faster. I'm in a hurry!"

Like the inebriated man, Nadab and Abihu were priests without a purpose. They were rushing into the tabernacle to do things without ever having given consideration to God's plan or God's schedule.

Also, in their haste and in their impulsive spirit, they trespassed into the holy place. Leviticus 16:1-2 seems to indicate that Nadab and Abihu were wrong not only as to the time but also as to the place. They should never have intruded beyond the veil. Trespassing into the holy place was strictly forbidden.

Are you operating within God's plan for your life? God has a divine schedule mapped out for your Christian growth. Are you maturing on schedule? Jesus said, "The Father has not left Me alone, for I always do those things that please him" (Jn 8:29). Do you always seek to please your heavenly Father? Nadab and Abihu did not give careful attention to adhering to the will of God. The result: a devouring fire!

4. They Manifested the Wrong Conduct

There is no way to be absolutely certain that strong drink prompted the thoughtless and unholy activities of Nadab and Abihu at the altar of incense. Nevertheless, God's warning to Aaron in Leviticus 10:9 suggests the probability. God said, "Do not drink wine or intoxicating drink, you, nor thy sons with you, when ye go into the tabernacle of meeting, lest ye die. It shall be a statute forever throughout your generations." Therefore, "if anyone cleanses himself from the latter (iniquity), he will be a vessel for honor, sanctified and useful for the Master, prepared for every good work" (2 Tm 2:21).

In keeping with God's instructions to Aaron, the believer-priest to-day must lift up a standard of righteousness for a world groping in darkness. He declares that we must be able to "distinguish between holy and unholy and between unclean and clean" (Lv 10:10).

Perhaps the apostle Paul had this Old Testament incident in mind when he wrote to the church in Ephesus, "Therefore, do not be unwise, but understand what the will of the Lord is. And do not be drunk with wine, in which is dissipation; but be filled with the Spirit" (Eph 5:17-18). God always has a better idea.

While man often substitutes the lesser for the better, God gives the better for the lesser. Strong drink gives a man red eyes, a yellow streak down his back, a blue outlook, and a dark brown breath. But the full-ness of the Holy Spirit will give to man a clear conscience and a pure heart. When the saint of God drinks in the fullness of the Holy Spirit, he has a hallelujah and not a hangover.

Tragically, Nadab and Abihu incurred the wrath of God. Perhaps they used the wrong fire or offered the wrong incense or employed the wrong schedule or manifested the wrong conduct, or perhaps they were wrong on all four counts. Consequently, God rained down His fire of retribution upon the two disobedient priests.

II. THE DESTRUCTION OF PRIESTS

Many people think of God as a benevolent, old grandfather who is tolerant of everything; however, the destruction of Nadab and Abihu disprove this theory. Their destruction makes two things absolutely clear.

1. Disobedience Is Serious

God responded immediately to the disobedience of these youthful priests. The Bible says, "So fire went out from the LORD and devoured them, and they died before the Lord" (Lv 10:2). It is foolish for a man to think that he can live in willful disobedience and rebellion toward the revealed will of God.

Consider some examples where the seriousness of disobedience is portrayed.

First, consider the occasion in 1 Samuel 13, where King Saul usurped the office of the priest. Saul was in a very precarious predicament. The people of Israel were scattered from him. The hostile Philistines were gathering around him. Samuel had failed to come at the appointed time to minister in the name of the Lord and to offer prayers of supplica-tion. Saul felt that if the Lord were not entreated to intervene in his behalf, the Philistines would utterly destroy him and the remnant that remained; therefore, he offered a burnt offering to the Lord.

When Samuel came upon the scene, he said to Saul, "You have done foolishly. You have not kept the commandment of the LORD your God, which he commanded you" (1 Sm 13:13). Saul had no right to function in the office of the priest. He was not of the tribe of Levi, the priestly tribe. He was of the tribe of Benjamin. Regardless of the circumstances, regardless of the apparent invasion of the Philistines, regardless of the absence of priests, Saul had no right to usurp the priest's office.

As the result of Saul's "foolishness," he was rejected by God as the king over Israel. The Lord said, "I greatly regret that I have set up Saul as king, for he has turned back from following Me, and has not performed My commandments" (1 Sm 15:11). The result? God took away the throne and stripped Saul's descendants of their kingly heritage.

If Saul wrongly assumed the office of the priest, if he sought to make supplication to the Lord, if he offered burnt offerings to the Lord, and if he kindled God's wrath against him, do you think God would be pleased with any believer-priest who refused to minister in the name of the Lord and render service in Jesus' name?

There is another interesting example of disobedience in 2 Samuel 6. The ark of the covenant was being transported from Gibeah to the city of David. The Kohathites were to transport the ark, according to the Word of God. The Kohathites responsible for transporting the ark to the city of David were Uzzah and Ahio. The Scripture tells us that when they came to Nachon's threshing floor, the cart hit a chuckhole and the ark of the covenant tipped to one side and that Uzzah took hold of it to keep it from falling. The Bible says, "Then the anger of the Lord was aroused against Uzzah; and God struck him there for his error; and he died there by the ark of God" (v. 7).

Many would say that God is unjust for striking a man dead for trying to preserve the ark of the covenant from falling to the ground and being crushed. But Uzzah, being a Kohathite, was trained from the time he was born to know how to transport the ark. The ark did not belong on a cart, not even a new cart, not any cart. Uzzah was well aware of the fact that he was not supposed to touch the ark under any circumstance. His disobedience caused the anger of the Lord to be kindled against him. Disobedience is serious business with God!

The New Testament records the example of the disobedience of Ananias and Sapphira. In Acts 5 this couple came to Peter and gave a portion of the money which they had received from the sale of real estate under the pretense of giving it all. Their hypocrisy and deceitfulness resulted in the Lord striking them dead at the very feet of the apostles. Disobedience is serious!

2. God Is Sovereign

The destruction of Nadab and Abihu also attests to the sovereignty of God. God is holy. God is just. Ultimately, God is going to do what He must do in order to preserve His righteousness and majesty.

All too often we want to reduce God to the limits of our little finite minds. Martin Luther once wrote, "Your thoughts of God are too human." But any time a sinner really sees the majesty of God, he has an overwhelming sense of fear because he knows he deserves to be consumed. God is synonymous with love, but the traditional concept of love is not compatible with the biblical concept of love.

Many today think of love as a syrupy, sentimental tolerance and acceptance of practically every philosophy and every kind of conduct. God's love is perfect and has discipline and chastisement in it. In Him is the perfect balance between love and justice!

Indeed, the Bible also declares that vengeance and fury belong to Him (Dt 32:39-41). The Scriptures avow that, "God is a just judge, and God is angry with the wicked every day" (Ps 7:11). God is angry against them because they are rebelling against His authority.

When Job saw a clear picture of the majesty of God, he said, "Therefore, I abhor myself, and repent in dust and ashes" (Jb 42:6).

When Simon Peter saw the miraculous power of the Lord, he fell down and said, "Depart from me; for I am a sinful man, O Lord!" (Lk 5:8).

When John, on the Isle of Patmos, saw the glorified Christ, he fell at His feet as though he were dead (Rv 1:17).

When Isaiah saw the holiness of God, he cried out, "Woe is me for I am undone!" (Is 6:5).

We need to recognize the holiness and the majesty of God. We need to recognize that He is an all-wise God who is perfect, who always does right, and who cannot make a mistake. The fire that was sent to destroy Nadab and Abihu gives a clear indication that these sons of Aaron placed a greater emphasis upon their privileges than upon their responsibilities.

Every believer must remember that he is accountable to a holy and just God, and that to "to whom much has been committed, of him they will ask the more" (Lk 12:48).

III. THE DEMEANOR OF PRIESTS

The attitude and conduct of Aaron are worthy of note. The Bible simply relates that "Aaron held his peace" (Lv 10:3). Moses further instructed family members not to mourn the death of Nadab and Abihu openly. He encouraged them to continue to fulfill their duties as the priests of God; therefore, from Aaron's family there was no mourning, no grief, no indication of resentment toward God. Rather there was a beautiful acceptance of God's righteous act. By their silence and unquestioning submission, they glorified God and exonerated His right to retribution.

The book of Joshua reveals a similar situation concerning Achan. Achan was the one who took the spoils of battle from Jericho. The spoils consisted of a beautiful Babylonian garment, two hundred shekels of silver, and a wedge of gold that weighed fifty shekels. Achan hid those treasures in his tent. Keeping those items was a sin against God. When he was confronted with this matter by Joshua, Achan confessed his sin. He confessed it all. Then do you know what happened? God had Achan killed.

It is difficult for people to comprehend the nature of a God who would do that, but because of Achan's confession God was able to do what he did and be exonerated. When Joshua confronted Achan, Joshua said, "Now Joshua said unto Achan, 'My son, I beg you, give glory to the LORD God of Israel, and make confession unto him; and tell me now what you have done; do not hide it from me" (Jo 7:19).

God is bound and determined to punish sin. God had to punish sin. God had to punish Achan's sin, and through his confession, God's justice was exonerated when the sentence for the sin was meted out. By the same token when Aaron and his family members did not speak out against God for His retribution upon Nadab and Abihu, God's justice was exonerated. In David's great confessional psalm, he said, "For I acknowledge my transgressions, and my sin *is* always before me. Against You, You only, have I sinned, and done *this* evil in Your sight—That You may be found just when You speak, *And* blameless when You judge" (51:3-4).

David knew that he had committed horrible, heinous sins. He knew that God hated sin. He knew that God could do nothing but punish sin. He knew that God had said, "Now therefore, the sword shall never depart from your house, because you have despised Me, and have taken the wife of Uriah, the Hittite, to be your wife' (2 Sm 12:10). Although Nathan had told David that he would not die (2 Sm 12:13), he knew that he was going to have to face the consequences of his sin, and, indeed, to his dying day David paid for his sin. The child born out of the adulterous relationship died. The son, Absalom, whom he wanted to succeed him as king also died. His family history is marked by sin, incest, death and sorrow. But David said, "I acknowledge my transgressions, I confess my sin, so that the world and generations to come will know that God is completely justified when he sends retribution and judgment upon me and my house" (see Ps 51:3-4).

Remember that every sin breeds a moral ulcer and every sin that is not repented of and placed under the blood of Jesus Christ will reap the wrath of an angry God. God wants to find everyone clothed in the righteousness of Jesus Christ. But because He is just, He cannot simply wink at our sins and smile at our iniquities. "Be not deceived; God is not mocked: for whatsoever a man sows, that shall he also reap" (Gal 6:7).

3

❧

The Mysterious Melchizedek (Hebrews 7:1-10)

A rather ambitious seminary student had been called to his first church. An ordination council was assembled to determine the suitability of this ecclesiastical neophyte for the ministry. In an effort to test him on his theological expertise, one venerable pastor spoke first, "Describe the order of the priesthood after Melchizedek." The nervous preacher-boy sheepishly replied, "Sir, if it's just the same to you, I'd rather tell you the story of David and Goliath."

Melchizedek is such an enigma that he is seldom the subject for sermons in our day. For the most part he has been relegated to the realm of obscurity, yet no study of the priesthood would be complete without a careful consideration of the mysterious Melchizedek. Although there is only a limited amount of information available concerning him, there is a significance about him which demands attention.

Melchizedek is mentioned in only three books of the Bible, yet his name is so strategically placed in the Word of God that the rarity of its appearance makes it strangely conspicuous. Melchizedek's appearance into human history is recorded in Genesis 14:18-20, at the time when he had an encounter with Abraham. Almost a thousand years later David made mention of him, declaring that the Messiah's priesthood would be after the order of Melchizedek (Ps 110:4).

After another millennium the writer of Hebrews, under the inspiration of the Holy Spirit, added knowledge of Melchizedek by giving an exposition of the Genesis passage concerning him (7:1-10). So, in essence, Melchizedek is introduced in Genesis, affirmed in the Psalms, and expounded upon in Hebrews.

These three accounts of Melchizedek in the Holy Scriptures provide remarkable evidence of the unity and the infallibility of the Word of God. Throughout the Bible we discover that approximately forty contributing writers relate the same thoughts, introduce the same revelations, reiterate the same incomparable truths. As W. A. Criswell declared, "What is enfolded in the Old Testament is unfolded in the New. What lies latent in the Old Testament is patent in the New."[1]

Indeed, the whole Bible fits together like a beautiful mosaic of truth. It is amazingly and astonishingly harmonious and coherent. It is divinely inspired, not only in its general intent but also in its most minute details. It is inspired, not only in its inclusions but also in its omissions. The information we have about Melchizedek has been supplied by three writers of Holy Scripture. They lived in three eras of history and wrote under vastly different circumstances; yet each writer confirmed and validated the information supplied by the others. The passages concerning Melchizedek present an excellent case for the verbal inspiration of the Scripture and the infallibility of the Word of God.

Dr. John H. Gerstner, noted Bible lecturer and author, is reported to have presented his case for the inerrancy of the Scriptures in a lecture at the Harvard Divinity School. His audience was not at all convinced that the Scriptures were without error. In an effort to emphasize his point, Dr. Gerstner said, "Dear Sirs, you would agree, would you not, with the statement, The Bible, which is the Word of God, errs'?" The group nodded their agreement. Then the esteemed lecturer said, "We will not do great violence to our thesis if we eliminate the words, 'the Bible which is...' What we now have is '...the Word of God errs.' Would you agree with the validity of that statement?" Those present voiced their concurrence. Dr. Gerstner then said, "What great difference would it make if we eliminated from our thesis the phrase, 'the Word of'? What we now have is the statement, 'God errs.' Can you agree with that?" The logic of Dr. Gerstner was driven home to the hearts of many of those who heard him that day.

To say that the Word of God errs is to say that the God of the Word errs. The record of Melchizedek gives substance to the amazing unity, harmony, and authenticity of Scripture.

I. THE IDENTITY OF MELCHIZEDEK

There is a mystery concerning the identity of Melchizedek. Scholars are not at all in agreement as to who this seemingly inscrutable personage really was. There are many contentions and speculations, however.

Hebrew tradition says that Melchizedek was simply a title given to Shem. Shem, the first son of Noah, apparently continued to worship the true God. Genesis 11:10-11 indicates that Shem lived 502 years after the flood. Thus, he would have been a contemporary of Abraham. Those who hold to this view declare that it provides a sufficient explanation of Hebrews 7:3, which describes Melchizedek, "Without father, without mother, without genealogy, having neither beginning of days, nor end of life."

In order to apply this verse to Shem, one must assume that it refers to the eternal priesthood after the order of Melchizedek with Adam as the first priest in this order and Christ as the last priest in this order, remembering that Shem was a descendant of Adam and Christ was a descendant of Shem. Adam, the first priest in this order, was not born and had neither father nor mother. Christ, the last priest in this order, had no descendant and His life is without end. Those who hold to the Hebrew tradition use this logic to describe an abiding priesthood.

Other scholars believe Melchizedek was a local Canaanite chieftain who was a type of Christ, even as Adam, Aaron, and the brazen serpent were types of Christ. Those who hold to this view agree that the terminology is descriptive of Christ, but they point to the phrase, "but made like the Son of God" (Heb 7:3) and say, "This indicates that he was not Christ but like Christ and, therefore, a type of Christ."

Others speculate that Melchizedek was some supernatural messenger, or mighty angel. The view has even been offered that Melchizedek was "the fallen Adam" from another planet sent to earth to behold the unfolding of God's plan of redemption for the fallen race of this world's Adam.

It appears, however, that the most accurate and trustworthy interpretation is that Melchizedek is a Christophany. *Christophany* comes from two Greek words: *Christos*, meaning "Christ," and *phaino*, meaning "to appear." So, the word Christophany signifies a corporal appearing of Christ, or a manifestation of Christ. This appearance of the Lord to Abraham is not at all unlike His manifestations to Jacob at Peniel (Gn 32:24-30), to Joshua at Jericho (Jo 5:14-15), and to Nebuchadnezzar in the fiery furnace (Dn 3:25). So, the appearance of Melchizedek to Abraham is a remarkable manifestation of the preincarnate Son of God.

Look at the name Melchizedek. The very word itself means "king of righteousness." *Melech* is Hebrew for "king" and *psedeo* is Hebrew for "righteousness." Jeremiah referred to our Lord as *Jehovah-Tsidkenu*, which means "Jehovah our righteousness" (Jer 23:6). Jeremiah also referred to the coming Christ a as "the Branch of righteousness" (33:15). In 1 John 2:1 our Savior is referred to as "Jesus Christ the righteous" (GNB). At His baptism Jesus declared that He came "to fulfil all righteousness" (Mt 3:15). Paul declared, "But of him you are in Christ Jesus, who became for us wisdom from God - and righteousness, and sanctification, and redemption" (1 Cor 1:30). Could not Melchizedek, the "king of righteousness," and Jesus Christ, "the righteous One," be one and the same?

Consider the purity and the holiness and the righteousness of our Great High Priest, Jesus Christ. The writer of Hebrews describes him as "holy, harmless, undefiled, separate from sinners, and has become higher than the heavens" (7:26). One can find fault with the preacher and glaring deficiencies in the church, but there stands One supreme. No man can point his finger at the Son of God and find a blemish in His character.

When Judas reviewed the life of Jesus and reconsidered his dastardly deed of betrayal, he cried out, "I have sinned by betraying innocent blood" (Mt 27:4). After Pilate had heard all of the accusations against Jesus, he declared, "I find no fault in him" (Jn 19:6). At the moment of Jesus' death, the centurion who beheld His agony on the cross said, "Certainly this was a righteous man" (Lk 23:47).

Yet the Bible declares that God took His pure, holy, innocent, only begotten Son and "made Him [Jesus] who knew no sin to be sin for us, that we might become the righteousness of God in him" (2 Cor 5:21).

To fully appreciate the fact that God imputed our sins upon Jesus Christ, we must understand God's attitude concerning sin. The Scriptures clearly state that God cannot bear to look upon sin and hates it with a heavenly passion. To a holy God sin is as grotesque as a buzzard sitting on the dining room table, as horrid as a rattlesnake in the infant's crib, and as deadly as rampaging cancer cells in the vital organs. Yet, God "made him who knew no sin to be sin for us." "It means 'He stood before God with all our sin upon him that we, through faith, might stand before God with none of our sin upon us.' He who was righteous was judged before God as unrighteous so that we who are unrighteous should be judged before God as righteous!"[2]

Having established the meaning and significance of the name Melchizedek, consider his position as the "King of Salem." *Salem* is a word that is closely kin to the common Hebrew word *shalom*, which means "peace." Incidentally, this is the first mention of "peace" in the Bible. Melchizedek is identified not only as the epitome of righteousness and the essence of peace, but also as the regent of both.

The view that this appearance of Melchizedek is a Christophany is enhanced by the fact that Jesus is referred to as the "Prince of Peace" (Is 9:6). The apostle Paul wrote that, "for He Himself [Jesus] is our peace" (Eph 2:14). Indeed, in Him is the "peace of God . . . which passes all understanding" (Phil 4:7). It was this peace that Jesus bequeathed to His disciples. He said, "Peace I leave with you, my peace I give unto you: not as the world gives do I give to you" (Jn 14:27). This inspired Word declares, "Of the increase of His government and peace there will be no end" (Is 9:7).

One of the beautiful examples of the peace of Christ is found in Mark 4:35-41, where it is recorded that a great storm of wind swept across the Sea of Galilee. Tempestuous waves came crashing against the side of the ship that contained Jesus and His disciples. The boat was quickly filling with water, and the disciples perceived that they were in great peril. In the midst of this time, when the sea was raging and the disciples were paralyzed with fear, Jesus was fast asleep. There was a divine serenity and an abiding peace about the Lord Jesus Christ that was inexplicable to the minds of the disciples. The peace that Jesus Christ gives is not dependent upon circumstances; it transcends circumstances. It is also a remarkably beautiful truth that the apex of righteousness and peace connects in Jesus Christ. "Surely His salvation is near to those who fear him; that glory may dwell in our land. Mercy and truth have met together; righteousness and peace have kissed" (Ps 85:9-10).

It is also interesting to note that there are certain irreversible, irrevocable patterns in the Bible. The Bible speaks of things in pairs, in groups; for example, the Bible declares, "Believe and be baptized." The Word of God never declares, "Be baptized and then believe." Infants cannot believe; therefore, we do not baptize infants. When the Ethiopian eunuch requested to be baptized, Philip said, "If thou believe with all your heart, you may" (Ac 8:37). God's order is to believe and then be baptized.

There is another significant biblical order that is irrevocable—repentance and faith. The scriptural order is not faith and repentance; it is always repentance and faith. Repentance must precede faith because repentance deals with sin, and sin is a mortal enemy to faith. The Bible says, "Beloved, if our heart does not condemn us, we have confidence toward God" (1 Jn 3:21).

Another significant coupling in the Bible is this matter of righteousness and peace. Peace never usurps the prior position of righteousness. First an individual is made "the righteousness of God in Him" (2 Cor 5:21). Then one becomes the possessor of Christ's imperturbable peace. Christ gives us peace by giving us righteousness. Charles Spurgeon explained:

There could be no true peace that was not grounded upon righteousness; and out of righteousness peace is sure to spring up... If there could be a kind of peace apart from righteousness it would be dank, dark, deadly, a horrible peace ending in a worse misery than war itself could inflict. It is needful where an unrighteous peace exists that it should be broken up, that a better peace should be established upon a true foundation which will last forever.[3]

To substantiate the Christophany of Melchizedek, one must note that he was "without father, without mother, without [genealogy], having neither beginning of days nor end of life" (Heb 7:3). Genesis, the book that introduces Melchizedek, gives meticulous care to genealogies and ancestral records. If he had had parents or children, the writer of Genesis would have violated an established pattern not to have recorded them. If there had been no ancestral record of Melchizedek, would not the writer of Hebrews have made mention of that rather than making the bold, declarative statement that he was "without father, without mother"?

It appears that the description of Hebrews 7:3 could only be true of the preincarnate Christ. Our Savior is everlasting, world without end. He said, "Before Abraham was, I AM" (Jn 8:58). He stretches from eternity past into eternity future. He is "the same yesterday and today, and forever" (Heb 13:8).

Everything seems to be changing. The landscape changes. Where there once were pastures and fields with flowers, there are now apartment complexes and shopping centers. Our circle of friends changes. Elderly people who once had a wide circle of friends find that today only a small segment of that circle is left. The economy changes. Nothing is more uncertain and volatile than the stock market and the value of the dollar. Physical life changes. Yesterday our parents were young and vibrant and strong. Today they are bent with years, feeble, and frail. Yesterday the hair of the husband was black and thick, but today it is as white as snow. Yesterday the house was filled with the noise of laughter and play as the children romped in the den, but now the silence that once was most ardently sought is a most unwelcome thing. The table once set for five or six is now set for two. In our world it seems that nothing is abiding but change. Jesus, however, is the eternal unchanging One. He is our Solid Rock. He "remains a priest continually" (Heb 7:3).

That Melchizedek was a mere man and the king of some Canaanite city, perhaps Jerusalem as some suppose, is really incredulous; for example, Jerusalem was probably inhabited by idolatrous and wicked Jebusites (2 Sm 5:6) at the time Melchizedek appeared. Does it seem reasonable that such a people would choose as king one who embodied righteousness and peace? Indeed, Daniel declares that "the Most High rules in the kingdom of men, gives it to whomever he will, and sets over it the lowest of men" (4:17).

Some say that the reference to Melchizedek as being made "like unto the Son of God" militates against the interpretation of this personage as a Christophany. However, many believe that the fourth man who appeared in the fiery furnace was a Christophany, yet his form was described as being "like the Son of God" (Dn 3:25). "There is also a sense in which the Word of God was made to be the Son of God when He became flesh so that until then in any of His preincarnate appearances He was only temporarily made like the Son of God as He would one day become permanently."[4]

Some people believe that if Christ is a priest after the order of Melchizedek, as the Bible declares (Ps 110:4), Melchizedek could not have been the preincarnate Christ. However, consider the composition of this unique priestly order. Who else could qualify to be a part of this superior priesthood? Furthermore, it makes little sense to imagine that there were only two men ever to qualify for this lofty order of priests: Melchizedek and Christ. The order of this priesthood was uniquely occupied by Christ, introduced by His preincarnate form under the name of Melchizedek, and presently occupied by Himself as the ruling, reigning, resurrected Lord.

The evidence seems to indicate that the mysterious Melchizedek was none other than the Son of God in preincarnate form.

II. THE ACTIVITY OF MELCHIZEDEK

Since the Hebrew 7 passage is an exposition of the account of Melchizedek in Genesis 14, we must turn to the first book of the Bible to determine the activity of Melchizedek.

In Genesis 14 is recorded the first mention of war in the Bible. A coalition of four powerful kings combined their forces and attacked the city of Sodom. Sodom was utterly defeated; and the enemy kings captured the king of Sodom and Abraham's nephew, Lot, and his family. When Abraham heard about Lot's captivity, he organized a small army of 318 trained servants. They promptly set out to retrieve Lot and his family and to recover the spoils of Sodom. The Scripture reports the amazing victory of Abraham and his men (Gn 14:16).

Abraham was wealthy; but he had an opportunity to increase his wealth by keeping the spoils of battle, to which he had a legal right. By keeping the spoils, however, he would have promoted his own prosperity through the misfortune of others. Undoubtedly, he had a soul struggle concerning this issue, even though he was a great man of faith. During this time of struggle, as Abraham dealt with the temptation to keep the spoils of battle, Melchizedek appeared. The Scripture asserts that he brought forth to Abraham "bread and wine" (v. 18).

This provision from the hands of Melchizedek speaks of more than just the sufficiency of Christ. Abraham and his men were fatigued and battle weary. The provision from the hands of Melchizedek supplied needed sustenance and refreshment. The Bible says, "And my God shall supply all your need according to his riches in glory by Christ Jesus" (Phil 4:19).

This timely provision is also an early preview of the elements which are an integral part of the Lord's Supper. There is the bread which reminds us of the broken body of Jesus. There is the wine which reminds us of the shed blood of our Savior. Abraham was met by Melchizedek who brought tokens of the sacrifice our Savior would make at Calvary. This is a part of the scarlet thread of redemption that runs throughout the Word of God, from beginning to end.

The activity of Melchizedek is not only as a benefactor through the giving of bread and wine to Abraham, the weary conqueror, but also as blesser, who said, "Blessed be Abram of God Most High, Possessor of heaven and earth" (Gn 14:19). Through this blessing Melchizedek simply reminded Abraham that he did not need to depend upon questionable deals to increase his wealth. In essence, he was saying, "Why be greedy and grasping over the perishable trinkets of Sodom when you have God who owns it all as your source of supply?"

God sent the king of Salem to Abraham in order to prepare him for his meeting with the king of Sodom. Upon the exodus of Melchizedek, the king of Sodom entered and said to Abraham, "Give me the persons and take the goods for yourself" (Gn 14:21). The king of Sodom represents this old world which would influence men to misappropriate their priorities and which would draw them away from the Lord. It actually sounds as if he is saying, "I will give you the goods of this world in exchange for your soul." It sounds much like the temptation of the devil to Jesus when he showed Him the kingdoms of the world and said, "All these things I will give You if You will fall down and worship me" (Mt 4:9). Of course, Jesus refused that temptation and later said, "For what profit is it to a man, if he gains the whole world, and loses his own soul? Or what will a man give in exchange for his soul?" (Mt 16:26). Perhaps the most tragic picture in all of the Bible is that of the rich young ruler sorrowfully going away from Jesus. His love for his possessions kept him out of the kingdom of God.

A man I knew in Jackson, Mississippi, upon becoming a Christian, immediately sold his boat, television, and a set of drums, which he had previously played at a nightclub. He took the money from the sale of these items and gave most of it to the church. With the remaining money he purchased a beautiful leather-bound study Bible and set of commentaries on the Word of God. He said, "I wanted to eliminate those things from my life that would discourage an intimate walk with God and translate them into that which would encourage consistent living."

Abraham faced such a dilemma. But because of the presence and blessing of Melchizedek, Abraham gave evidence that he preferred the eternal to the temporal and the celestial to the terrestrial. In fact, I believe Melchizedek inspired Abraham to say to the king of Sodom, "I will take nothing, from a thread to a sandal strap, and that I will not take any thing that is yours, lest you should say, I have made Abram rich" (Gn 14:23). The battle Abraham won at this point was greater than his battle over the four enemy kings. He had won the battle over himself. He had won the battle over possessions.

I am reminded of a comment attributed to Mark Twain who was rebuking a man for his envy of the wealth of Andrew Carnegie. The critical man said in a condescending voice, "But I suppose like all the other millionaires Carnegie's money is tainted."

"Oh yes, "said Twain, with a wry smile, "'Taint yours and 'taint mine."

Mark Twain was absolutely right. None of it belongs to us. It all belongs to God. He is the owner, and He measures out a portion of it to us now and again, just to check upon the quality of our stewardship.

In the Word of God, the activity of Melchizedek is apparent. He operated in the life of Abraham as both a benefactor and a blesser. Similarly, Jesus desires to bless you and give to you. He said, "Come unto me...and I will give you..." (Mt 11:28).

III. THE SUPERIORITY OF MELCHIZEDEK

The primacy of Melchizedek is apparent in that the Bible states, "The lesser [Abraham] is blessed by the better [Melchizedek]"(Hebrews 7:7). Our text also indicates that Abraham paid tithes to Melchizedek, an indication of his superiority. This means that through Abraham, their progenitor, the entire Levitical priesthood who received tithes also paid tithes to Melchizedek. If Abraham, the greatest patriarch of his day, the fountainhead of the Chosen People of God, the "friend of God," and "the father of the faithful" paid tithes to Melchizedek, does that not speak of a superior priesthood? Actually, Melchizedek reveals the supreme and sovereign priesthood of Jesus Christ.

A careful study of Melchizedek also gives a new and fresh scriptural validity to the tithe. Some people say that the tithe is for the Jew and that it was established under the law. They contend that in the age of grace the principles of the law are minimized, if not completely nullified. I declare that if a Christian would not do more under grace than a Jew would do under the law, he is a disgrace to grace.

The story of Melchizedek teaches us that the principle of tithing is an eternal principle. It predates the law, it continued throughout the dispensation of the law, and it still continues in this day of grace. In Melchizedek there is a revelation of the unchanging and eternal priesthood of our Savior. Therefore, we, as Abraham's spiritual descendants, must render to our High Priest honor and worship by bringing our tithes to Him, that we may show forth our obedience to this eternal command.

The principle of the tithe is so indelibly written into the Word of God that the non-tither is considered a robber of God. The Bible declares, "Will a man rob God? Yet you have robbed me! But you say, In what way have we robbed You? In tithes and offerings" (Mal 3:8).

As a young boy, I remember quite distinctly an experience I had one Monday morning while walking to school. I occasionally altered my route from home to school for the sake of variety. On this particular Monday morning, my path carried me through the property of my home church, the First Baptist Church of Valdese, North Carolina. As I was walking between the worship center and the education building of our church, I saw a large box which I recognized as the church safe. It was, indeed, out of place in the churchyard; and, upon closer inspection, I observed that the door to the safe was ajar.

In a matter of moments others arrived on the scene. Church leaders and the police concluded that robbers had entered the church during the night, found the safe, somehow carted it into the church courtyard, pried open the door, and taken all the money from Sunday's offering.

The questions, the investigations, and the manhunt that followed were an amazement to me. I could not believe that anyone would forcibly break into the church office, vandalize the house of God, and steal the offerings which the believers had brought to give to the Lord. In my mind it was incredible that such a thing could ever happen.

Yet Sunday by Sunday church members who presumably have trusted their very souls into the hands of the living God refuse to trust Him with a dime out of every dollar and, thus, rob Him of that which is rightfully His.

In many affluent churches I have an idea that members drive to church in stolen cars, wear stolen designer clothing, and bedeck themselves with stolen accessories; then they leave church, go to a fine restaurant, eat a sumptuous meal, and pay for it with stolen money. The stolen goods and the stolen money came from the tithes which these people withheld from God.

Of course, the tithe is the beginning point in the life of faith. Those who have proven themselves good stewards in the lowly realm of material things will have opportunities to advance in God's school of faith according to their faithfulness in each level of testing. Those who have graduated from the kindergarten level of the tithe will have an opportunity to move on to the elementary level of stewardship, and then to the high-school level, and ultimately to the university level where there is an opportunity for a Ph.D. in the principles of stewardship. The graduates of this level will be entrusted with "the true riches" which some have interpreted to be the power of the Holy Spirit. Jesus said, "He who is faithful in what is least is faithful also in much: and he who is unjust in what is least is unjust also in much. Therefore, if you have not been faithful in the unrighteous mammon, who will commit to your trust the true riches?" (Lk 16:10-11).

Melchizedek, the preincarnate Christ of God, received tithes from Abraham and, thus, from all of the Levites and all of those who stood in the priestly order of the Old Testament. He embodied the eternal principle of the tithe. Herein is evidence of his superiority.

IV. THE DYNASTY OF MELCHIZEDEK

In Melchizedek, this Old Testament Christophany, there is an eschatological picture of the millennial glory of Christ when "He shall be a priest on his throne" (Zec 6:13) and rule the earth in righteousness and peace from the earthly city of Jerusalem.

Isaiah spoke of the Lord Jesus Christ when he said, "Of the increase of His government and peace there will be no end, upon the throne of David, and over his kingdom, to order it and establish it with judgment and justice from that time forward, even forever. The zeal of the Lord of hosts will perform this" (Is 9:7). Where was the throne of David? It was in Jerusalem. Remember that Melchizedek means "king of righteousness." He is the king of Salem or the king of Jerusalem. The combination of righteousness, peace, and Jerusalem produces an image of the millennial kingdom.

One day Jesus will set up His millennial kingdom and rule in righteousness from the throne of David in Jerusalem. In Melchizedek we have a revelation of that coming day.

Finally, consider the fact that Melchizedek is described as "the priest of God Most High" (Gn 14:18). This is a title which transcends all national and sectarian limitations. This title represents a marked contrast between Aaron's priesthood and the priesthood of Melchizedek. The priestly ministry of Aaron was confined to the limits of Israel, but the priesthood of Melchizedek represented a more inclusive and a more comprehensive ministry because he functioned as the "God Most High, Possessor of heaven and earth" (v. 19). This title seems to present a perfect picture of the thousand-year reign of Christ. It is written,

> Behold, the days are coming, says the Lord, that I will raise to David a Branch of righteousness, a King shall reign and prosper, and execute judgment and justice in the earth. In his days

Judah will be saved, and Israel will dwell safely; Now this is
his name by which He will be called, THE LORD OUR
RIGHTEOUSNESS (Jer 23:5-6).

The blessed contemplation is that every believer-priest will have
the opportunity and responsibility of ruling and reigning with Christ
on earth for one thousand years. In fact, the Scripture clearly states,
"They shall be priests of God and of Christ, and shall reign with Him a
thousand years" (Rv 20:6).

We live in a time of violence and hatred and variance between races
and classes of people. But the day is coming when violence will end,
and class strife and hatred will be history. Truly Melchizedek, "the
King of Jerusalem," "the Prince of Peace," will establish his dynasty
from Jerusalem and rule and reign on earth in a glorious millennial
kingdom. He, as the preincarnate Christ, represents a ruling priesthood that abides forever.

Notes

1. W. A. Criswell, *The Bible for Today's World* (Grand Rapids: Zondervan Publishing House, 1965), p. 32.
2. R. G. Lee, *Grapes From Gospel Vines* (Nashville: Broadman Press, 1976), p. 22.
3. Charles Haddon Spurgeon, *Treasury of the Bible, Vol. 4, New Testament* (Grand Rapids: Zondervan Publishing House, 1968), p. 82.
4. Henry Morris, *Commentary on Genesis* (Grand Rapids: Baker Book House, 1976), p. 321.

4

Christ, Our Superior Priest
(Hebrews 7:11-28)

The Levitical priesthood was but a shadow of the superior
priesthood to come. As a flickering torch predated the flu-
orescent light, as the horse-drawn surrey preceded the automobile, and
as the phonograph was the forerunner of the MP3 and MP4 players, so
was the Levitical priesthood the prototype of the preeminent priesthood of Jesus Christ.

The priesthood of the Aaronic order could not effectively pacify the
conscience, cleanse the heart, or provide access to God. In fact, the
priesthood of the old covenant simply offered an umbrage, a hint of the
coming, complete, continuing, capable, consecrated priesthood of the
Lord Jesus Christ. To sufficiently understand the significance and the
superiority of the priesthood of the Son of God, one must first consider
the prototype.

I. THE PREVIOUS PRIESTHOOD

Our text reveals several glaring deficiencies in the Old Testament, or previous priesthood. Indeed, this priesthood was incomplete, inferior, and invalidated.

1. It Was Incomplete

The reality that the Old Testament priesthood was incomplete or imperfect is clearly delineated in the text. Two words found in Hebrews 7:11 substantiate this truth: "perfection" and "another." "Therefore, if perfection were through the Levitical priesthood, [for under it the people received the law,] what further need was there that another priest should rise according to the order of Melchisedek, and not be called according to the order of Aaron?"

The word "perfection" in this verse is a translation of the Greek word *teleiosis*, meaning to finish, to bring to completion. In Hebrews the word seems to refer to the producing of a satisfactory relationship whereby man is able to enter into the presence of God and stand before Him in good favor.

The old covenant could not provide this kind of free access to God. This right of way to the Father could only be accomplished by Christ who said, "No man comes to the Father except through me" (Jn 14:6). So, the Levitical priesthood was incomplete, imperfect.

Of course, God never intended for the Levitical priesthood to continue forever. God never removes or abolishes any institution or ordinance without introducing something that is incomparably more excellent. So, with the appearance of Melchizedek in Genesis 14, God introduced a new priestly order. The superiority of that order with Christ as its focal point is predicted in Psalm 110. Indeed, if the Levitical priesthood had been completely satisfactory, there would have been no need for a new priestly order.

Under the old sacrificial system, administered by the Levitical priesthood, sins were covered but not removed. There was a measure of forgiveness, but it was never completely efficacious. Complete forgiveness and total access to God are possible only through Jesus Christ. "For by one offering He has perfected forever those who are being sanctified. . . .Therefore, brethren, having boldness to enter the Holiest by the blood of Jesus, by a new and living way which He consecrated for us, through the veil, that is, His flesh, and *having* a High Priest over the house of God, let us draw near with a true heart in full assurance of faith" (Heb 10:14,19-22). If imperfection and incompleteness come by sin, then completion, perfection, and access come by the once-and-for-all sacrifice of Jesus Christ and His righteousness.

There is also the mention of the need for "another priest" (Heb 7:11). In the Greek language there are two words for "another": *allos* and *heteros*. The word *allos* signifies another of the same kind; for example, when Jesus gave His upper room discourse to the disciples, He said, "And I will pray the Father and He will give you another Helper (Comforter -*allon parakleton*], that he may abide with you forever" (Jn 14:16). Jesus was referring to the Holy Spirit who would be another of like kind, having essentially the same attributes of Christ Himself.

The Greek word *heteros* denotes "another of a different kind"; for example, Stephen declared, "Another king arose, who did not know Joseph" (Ac 7:18). The word *heteros* in this passage signifies a king not like his predecessor. In Galatians, Paul warned the church about her drift toward a "different gospel" (1:6). *Heteros* here indicates a gospel totally different from the gospel proclaimed by the apostle Paul.

So, in speaking of "another priest," the writer of Hebrews used the word *heteros*, denoting "another of a different kind." In the new priestly order, the eternal would replace the temporal; the divine would supplant the physical; and the perfect, the complete, would abrogate the incomplete.

2. It Was Inferior

The emergence of another (*heretos*) priesthood points to the inferiority of the preceding order. God's Word declares, "For if that first covenant had been faultless, then no place would have been sought for the second" (Heb 8:7). There is further substantiation for this concept from the inspired Word, "He takes away the first that he may establish the second" (Heb 10:9). The sharp contrast between the first and the second priesthood is clearly delineated in Hebrews 7:15-17. The Scripture emphatically states, "There arises another priest" (v. 15). The terminology suggests the extraordinary and dramatic arrival of a different kind of priest.

The priest of the new covenant is made "not according to the law of a fleshly commandment, but according to the power of an endless life" (v. 16). Consider the contrast between "law" (*nomon*) and "power" (*dunamis*).

The primary objective of the law is to regulate life and restrain life. To the church in Galatia Paul wrote, "But before faith came, we were kept in custody under the law, being shut up to the faith which was later to be revealed. Therefore, the Law has become our tutor to lead us to Christ, that we may be justified by faith" (Gal 3:23-24, NASB). The life of the rich, young ruler was restrained, regulated, and kept in custody under the law. The Lord questioned him concerning his faithfulness to the Commandments. Although he failed to apply the directive of the Tenth Commandment to his life, he avowed, "All these things have I kept from my youth up: what do I still lack?" (Mt 19:20). He knew something was missing. The law had fulfilled its purpose in bringing him to Christ. The law does not suffice as our Savior; however, it is our signpost to the Savior.

Standing in contradistinction to the law which restrains is "the power"(*dunamis*) which enables. The English words *dynamic* and *dynamite* come from the Greek word *dunamis*. The original word signifies a certain impetus, an incentive, a causative force. In 1 Corinthians 1:24, Christ, our High Priest, is described as the *dunamis* of God. In truth He has the power, the dynamic, to save, to succor, to sanctify, to secure, and to sympathize with all those who will come to Him. Because He is fully God, He has the power to represent God to man. Because He is fully man, He has the power to represent man to God. Moreover, the new priesthood embodies the *dunamis* of an endless life.

The inferiority of the Levitical priesthood and the superiority of the priesthood of Christ are made plain in Hebrews 7:19: "For the law made nothing perfect, on the other hand, there is the bringing in of a better hope, through which we draw near to God." This divine word emphasizes the inability of the old versus the capability of the new.

3. It Was Invalidated

The Levitical priesthood was a part of the law established under the old covenant. Since the law was "weak through the flesh" (Rm 8:3), since the law was unprofitable, since it made nothing perfect, God annulled it (Heb 7:18). The word *disannulled* comes from *athetesis*, which means "to invalidate, to nullify, to set aside." The validity of the Melchizedekian priesthood invalidates the Levitical priesthood.

On April 9, 1865, General Robert E. Lee surrendered to General Ulysses S. Grant at Appomattox, Virginia. With this surrender of the South to the North, the War Between the States ended. The war settled two important issues: (1) No state could secede from the union again, and (2) never again would slavery exist in the United States. Once again, the Confederate states were incorporated into the life and framework of the Union (United States).

The surrender of General Lee nullified the Confederacy. The presidency of Jefferson Davis over the South was made void. The controversial rebel flag, still a cherished memento of the past to many Southerners, was replaced by the Stars and Stripes. Confederate money was invalidated, and the currency of the Union became the bona fide monetary exchange.

Similarly, the advent of the new priesthood invalidated the old. Under the old covenant, the blood sacrifices covered over sin, but they could not remove sin. There was a measure of forgiveness, but it was never complete. The ministry of the old priesthood previewed the emancipation proclamation, but under the new priesthood every slave of sin can be set free by the precious blood of Jesus Christ. In the establishment of the new, which is perfect, there is no longer a need for the old. The preceding priesthood is annulled, made void, invalidated.

II. THE PREEMINENT PRIESTHOOD

The Bible tells us that "man has no advantage (preeminence)" (Eccl 3:19). The same word of God proclaims that Jesus is the head of the church, "who is the beginning, the firstborn from the dead; that in all things He might have the preeminence" (Col 1:18). The preeminence of Christ obviously carries over into His priesthood.

1. The Surety of This Priesthood

The writer of Hebrews declared, "By so much more Jesus has become a surety [egguos] of a better covenant" (Heb 7:22). This is the only time *egguos* occurs in the New Testament. This Greek word means "a guarantee" or "a pledge." *Egguos* could refer to someone who becomes the surety for a debt, signing his name as a guarantee that the bank note will be paid. The word could refer to a bondsman, who pledges his name, his wealth, his influence that a certain thing will be done. Concerning the new priestly order, Jesus is the guarantee of its superiority and effectiveness.

The meaning of "surety" is beautifully illustrated in the Old Testament Book of Genesis. In the day that Joseph was the prime minister over Egypt, a famine covered the whole earth. Joseph, however, anticipating the famine, filled the storehouses of Egypt with a surplus of corn. The brothers of Joseph, operating under the directive of their father, Jacob, went into Egypt to buy food to sustain them in their time of want. Joseph insisted that when they came for additional food that it would be necessary for them to bring their youngest brother, Benjamin, in order to prove their integrity. Since Joseph's brothers did not recognize him, they bore the news concerning Benjamin to their father with fear and trepidation.

When it came time to go into Egypt for more corn, Judah avowed to his father that he would become a surety for Benjamin. He said, "Send the lad with me, and we will arise and go, that we may live and not die, both we and you and also our little ones. I myself will be surety for him; from my hand you shall require him. If I do not bring him back to you and set him before thee, then let me bear the blame for ever" (Gn 43:8-9). History records the absolute faithfulness of Judah to his promise.

When Joseph saw Benjamin, he devised a plan to have Benjamin remain with him in Egypt. He had his silver chalice planted in Benjamin's sack of grain. Joseph had his steward to search the sacks of grain which had been given to the sons of Jacob. When the chalice was found in Benjamin's sack, it appeared that the sons of Jacob would have to return to their father without his youngest and most beloved son.

When it appeared that Benjamin was going to be kept in Egypt as a servant of Joseph, all the brothers returned with Benjamin to Joseph's house. Judah was the spokesman, declaring that he had pledged to his father that he would be a surety for Benjamin. His appeal to Joseph is one of the most plaintive pleas in all of the Word of God. Hear Judah's plea:

> Now therefore, when I come to your servant my father, and the lad *is* not with us, since his life is bound up in the lad's life, it will happen, when he sees that the lad *is* not *with us,* that he will die. So, your servants will bring down the gray hair of your servant our father with sorrow to the grave. For your servant became surety for the lad to my father, saying, 'If I do not bring him *back* to you, then I shall bear the blame before my father forever.' Now therefore, please let your servant remain instead of the lad as a slave to my lord, and let the lad go up with his brothers. For how shall I go up to my father if the lad *is* not with me, lest perhaps I see the evil that would come upon my father? (Gn 44:30-34).

Even as Judah became the guarantee to his father that Benjamin would be returned safely to Canaan, even so is Jesus the guarantee "of a better covenant" (Heb 7:22). This better testament, this perfect priesthood, guarantees that our sins will be removed, not just covered, that we have a continual advocate with the Father, and that our salvation is eternally secure.

2. The Steadfastness of This Priesthood

In contrasting the temporal priesthood of the old covenant to the eternal priesthood under the new covenant, the writer of Hebrews said, "Also there were many priests, because they were prevented by death from continuing. But He, because He continues forever, has an unchangeable priesthood." (Heb 7:23-24).

In Aaron the Israelites had a high priest who was temporary and imperfect. To demonstrate the temporal nature of the Aaronic priesthood, God commanded Aaron to die in front of the congregation of Israel (see Nm 20:25-29).

When Aaron died, the people of God suffered a traumatic experience. They mourned for Aaron for thirty days. Aaron had played a significant role in the life of the Israelites. He had often served as Moses' spokesman. As the high priest he had appeared before God on behalf of the people, and he had appeared before the people on behalf of God. He had made sacrifices to atone for the sins of the Israelites. The death of Aaron greatly affected the people of God.

Other high priests in the Levitical order likewise ministered in the tabernacle of old. But in each case their service was terminated. None could continue in the office of priest after becoming fifty years of age. They were all mortal men who died in their successive generations. The Bible declares that "they truly were many priests." According to Josephus, the Jewish historian, there were eighty-three high priests. Aaron, of course, was the first, and the last was Phannias, who was made high priest during the war that ended with the destruction of the Temple in AD 70.

Conversely, Jesus Christ, our Great High Priest, has a continuing, steadfast priesthood. The Greek word for unchangeable is *aparabaton*. This is a legal term. It means unalterable. When a judge reaches his decision and hands down a sentence, it must remain unalterable, inviolable. The priesthood of Christ, which makes Him the one and only mediator between God and man, is also unalterable. This new and better priesthood is unchanging and nontransferable. It is more steadfast than the laws of the universe, including the law of gravity, the law of inertia, and the law of centrifugal force. It is surer than the Rock of Gibraltar, the ebb and flow of the tides, and the sun rising in the east and setting in the west. It is as steadfast as the love and mercy of the Heavenly Father.

Our Great High Priest has no predecessor, and He will have no successor "because he continues forever, [and] has an unchangeable priesthood" (Heb 7:24). Some tend to think that when the final curtain is drawn on earth's history, and the elect of God are in the safe harbor of their heavenly home, there will be no need for Jesus to function as High Priest. However, in Revelation's futuristic view of Christ, He is dressed in priestly robes and even then, the redeemed of the Lord stand accepted before God in Him. He came to earth to acquire salvation for us; He ascended to the right hand of the Father to maintain it. Thus, we see the steadfastness of this priesthood, both now and forever.

3. The Salvation of This Priesthood

The writer of Hebrews affirmed that Jesus, our Great High Priest, is able to save to the uttermost (Heb 7:25). His ability to save is predicated upon the surety and the steadfastness of His priesthood.

The priests of the Old Testament were never able to save or administer a rite that resulted in salvation for anyone. They killed rams and bulls, goats and calves, pigeons and turtledoves. The blood of these sacrificial animals was sprinkled around the altar. The victims were cut into many pieces. These animal offerings were burned upon the altar before the Lord.

For hundreds of years animals were led to the slaughter to be sacrificed to a just and holy God. Rivers of blood were spilled for those who wanted to be absolved from their sins. The hope was that the shedding of blood would atone for sin and restore the sinner to a full and intimate fellowship with God. Nevertheless, all the animals that were killed and all the sacrifices that were offered and all the blood that was shed did not remove one sin or set one person completely right before the God of heaven. "And every priest stands ministering daily and offering repeatedly the same sacrifices, which can never take away sins: but this Man [Jesus], after he had offered one sacrifice for sins forever, sat down at the right hand of God" (Heb 10:11-12). Indeed, the old sacrificial system was but "a shadow of good things to come" (v. 1). That which was a shadow in the Old Testament reaches the glory of high noon in Jesus Christ.

Jesus, however, is able to do what other priests could simply preview. The Word of God tells us that "he is able even to subdue all things unto Himself" (Phil 3:21). Paul declared "that he is able to keep what I have committed unto Him until that Day" (2 Tm 1:12). In the Bible we are told that, "He is able to aid those that are tempted" (Heb 2:18). Now we read that "he is able to save to the uttermost those who come unto God through Him" (Heb 7:25). There is no limit to the ability of our Savior.

Jesus is able to save because His blood is completely efficacious. Charles Spurgeon said, "Morality may keep you out of jail, but it takes the blood of Jesus Christ to keep you out of hell." Nothing else will suffice for the removal of sin. Jeremiah said, "For though you wash yourself with lye, and use much soap, yet your iniquity is marked before Me, says the Lord God" (Jer 2:22).

Shakespeare emphasized the lingering stain of Lady Macbeth's murderous deed. She looks at the blood of Duncan upon her hands as she says, "What! will these hands ne'er be clean?... Here's the smell of blood still: all the perfumes of Arabia will not sweeten this little hand. Oh! oh! oh!"¹ Only the blood of Jesus can take a life that is stained and maimed by sin and make it clean and pure.

We are told that gold is the most precious of metals. For years men sought a solution that would dissolve this precious metal. At last, a solution of nitric acid and hydrochloric acid was concocted and put to the test of dissolving this precious metal. It was discovered that this solution would dissolve gold. This combination of acids came to be known as *aqua regia*, or royal water, because for years it was believed to be the only solution that could master gold.

There is only one thing that will dissolve and remove the sin stains of the human heart. The solution to sin pollution is the blood of Jesus Christ. The blood which the Lord Jesus shed upon Calvary's cross does not merely cover sin; it cleanses sin.

Furthermore, when Jesus saves people, He saves them completely and forever. This seems to be the double meaning of the word "uttermost." The word suggests both quality and quantity.

Salvation is often spoken of in three tenses: past, present, and future. The past tense suggests salvation from the *penalty* of sin. The present tense suggests salvation from the *power* of sin. The future tense suggests salvation from the very *presence* of sin.

As the Great High Priest, Jesus is keenly interested in delivering the sinner from sin in all of its tenses. There is much talk about the finished work of Christ on Golgotha. But there is much to be said about the unfinished work of Christ in glory. The efficacious death of Christ saves us from the penalty of sin. The enabling life of Christ saves us from the power of sin. The entreating intercessions of Christ will one day save us from the presence of sin. The Lord Jesus Christ will not cease to intercede in our behalf until the task is finished and He can present His own to the Father, "a glorious church, not having spot, or wrinkle or any such thing, but that she should be holy and without blemish" (Eph 5:27). Ultimately the task of our Lord will be completed. What began as salvation will end in glorification. At last, every believer will be conformed to the image of the Son of God. This is the goal—to populate heaven with people who are like Jesus Christ.

Since every believer is ultimately to be conformed to the image of Jesus Christ, consider next the attributes of the Son of God.

4. The Sanctification of This Priesthood

Since the new priestly order is embodied in Jesus Christ, His attributes set the standard for every believer-priest. He is not only our salvation but also our example. His priesthood sets forth not only the doctrine of justification but also the doctrine of sanctification. Consider the terminology used to describe the purity of our High Priest: "for such an High Priest was fitting for us, who is holy, harmless, undefiled, separate from sinners, and has become higher than the heavens" (Heb 7:26).

The writer of Hebrews declared that Jesus "is holy." *Hosios* is the Greek word translated "holy." This word seems to convey one special thought. It describes the individual who is pure in heart before God.

Jesus never had one spot on His life to indicate that He was a part of fallen humanity. Every other soul has been conceived in sin and shaped in iniquity. However, the Son of man, from the moment of His miraculous birth to the moment of His agonizing death, was always exemplary in His conduct, forever above reproach, and consistently well pleasing in His Father's sight.

Jesus went through the weaknesses peculiar to childhood, the temptations that befall adolescents, the peer pressure of teenagers, and progressed right through to manhood with His entire life submitted to the will and the way of God. His thoughts, His words, His deeds were in conformity to the wishes of His Heavenly Father. He could truthfully say, "For I do always those things that please Him" (Jn 8:29). And God could behold the life of His only begotten Son upon earth and declare, "This is my beloved Son, in whom I am well pleased" (Mt 17:5).

There have been seasons in my life when neither my earthly father nor my Heavenly Father could have been pleased with my conduct. I remember the spring of one year when I hit a baseball through the windshield of a neighbor's car and ran from the scene of the crime. I painfully recall the summer that I threw my uncle's best harness into the well. It was in the autumn of one of my boyhood years that I set the field of broom sedge on fire and then lied about who did it. One winter I was so bad I didn't think I would get anything but switches for Christmas.

In every season of every year, some iniquity has crept into my heart which has caused God to hide His face from me. Jesus never had that problem. Between Jesus and His Father there was always perfect accord.

Jesus is not only holy, which speaks of His relationship to God, but also *harmless*. This word pertains to His relationship to others. *Harmless* is the translation of the compound Greek word *akakos*. *Kakia* means evil, malicious, wicked. It can refer to a moral malignancy or depravity.

Oftentimes when the letter *a* is used as the prefix of a word, it serves as a contradiction; for example, *muse* means to study, to think, to deliberate. People go to a museum to study and reflect upon works of art. By putting an *a* in front of *muse*, the word becomes *amuse*. *Amuse* refers to a time of levity and jocularity which requires no thinking or deliberation.

The musical term *cappella* signifies the music of a choir with an orchestra or instrumental accompaniment. *Acappella* denotes a vocal chorus without instrumental accompaniment. The word *moral* means to conform to a standard of what is good and right. *Amoral* identifies the kind of behavior that has no sense of moral responsibility.

When an *a* is added to *kakos* as a prefix, it signifies the very opposite of evil and depravity and wickedness. This compound word fittingly describes Jesus because He is the antithesis of evil and depravity. He is the exact opposite of anything that is vile and wicked.

As the harmless Lamb of God, Jesus gave Himself in service to others. He dedicated Himself to lifting and encouraging even the weakest and most fragile of people. The Bible says, "A bruised reed He will not break, and smoking flax He will not quench" (Mt 12:20). His life was forever a stepping-stone, never a stumbling block. The Great High Priest of the new order is described also as "undefiled." The Greek word here is *amiantos*. Once again, the prefix a negates the meaning of the root word. *Miano* means to pollute, to contaminate, to defile. *Amiantos* refers to that which is free from pollution or defilement.

"For we do not have a High Priest who cannot sympathize with our weaknesses, but was in all *points* tempted as *we are*, *yet* without sin" (Heb 4:15). Jesus did not live in isolation from the profane, the immoral, and the corrupt people of society. He was personally confronted by the devil himself and tempted along the lines of the body, the soul, and the spirit. Yet the Son of God came through every trial and temptation without one mark of defilement upon Him. In fact, when Jesus touched the lepers, His purity overruled their contamination, and the lepers were cleansed.

The text describes Christ as "separate from sinners." This terminology is not an attempt to negate the full humanity of Jesus. He was as fully man as though He were not God and as fully God as though He were not man. Indeed, He was the epitome of manhood at its highest and best.

Yet Jesus had the capacity to live in the world and not be of the world. The holiness of Christ was not the mere negative innocence that results from a strict isolation from evil, but the positive holiness that confronts evil and conquers it.

The believer-priest can never be separate from sinners as is Jesus, our Great High Priest. Every believer is a sinner, saved by grace. Nevertheless, the call to every child of God is to "come out from among them, and be separate" (2 Cor. 6:17). The Christian is to stand out in this dark world like a diamond in a coal mine. The church cannot blame the world for being unregenerate, but the world can blame the church for being unholy. Every believer should give ample evidence that he is a "new creature."

The priesthood of every believer takes its cue from the Great High Priest, the Lord Jesus Christ. His life is the pattern for every believer. The First Epistle of John challenges us over and over again with the phrase, "as he is." John urged every believer to "walk in the light as He is in the light" (1:7). Once again, the child of God is encouraged "to walk just as He walked" (2:6). There is also the admonition for the saint of God to purify himself "just as He is pure" (3:3). Every member of the family of faith is also admonished to be righteous "just as He is righteous" (v. 7). The believer-priest, by the power of the Holy Spirit, is to emulate the example of Jesus Christ.

John Owen said:

> If we give up ourselves to the conduct of this High Priest, if by Him alone we design to approach unto God, then conformity unto Him in holiness of nature and life ac-

cording to our measure is indispensably required of us. None can more dishonor the Lord Christ, no more perniciously deceive and betray their own souls, than by professing Him to be their priest, with their trust thereby to be saved by Him, and yet not endeavor to be holy, harmless, undefiled, separate from sinners, like unto Him.[2]

The text also declares that Jesus was "made higher than the heavens." However, for the suffering of death, Jesus "was made a little lower than the angels" (Heb 2:9). In His condescension, He "made Himself of no reputation, taking the form of a bondservant, and coming in the likeness of men" (Phil 2:7). In His vicarious death on the cross, He was made "to be sin for us" (2 Cor 5:21). He was also made a curse for us (Gal 3:13). In His humiliation, Jesus even found it necessary to descend "into the lower parts of the earth" (Eph 4:9). However, the humiliation of Jesus and the sacrificial offering of Himself upon the cross for sinful men earned for Him the right to ascend to the position of honor at the right hand of the Father. Having dutifully discharged the principal part of His priestly office by His obedience unto death, Jesus has been highly exalted by God. Jesus has been given a name above every name. He is Lord!

5. The Sacrifice of This Priesthood

The death of Jesus on the cross was the one sacrifice sufficient for all people for all time. Concerning Jesus, our High Priest, the Bible says, "Who does not need daily, as those high priests, to offer up sacrifices, first for his own sins and then for the people's, for this He did once for all when He offered up Himself" (Heb 7:27).

Surely the Old Testament priests became weary with the offering of sacrifices. Their lives were filled with an unending ritual of ministering around bloody altars. For example, on the great Day of Atonement the high priest would kill a sacrifice and offer the blood of that sacrifice as an atonement for his sins. Upon having completed that task, the high priest would kill a lamb and take the blood of the lamb within the veil into the holy of holies. In the holy of holies there was the ark of the covenant. There was the mercy seat. On this one day of the year the high priest would pour the blood of the lamb upon that mercy seat. In this act an atonement for the sins of the people was made for one year.

The Bible says that Jesus Christ came into this world to be offered up as the sacrifice for sinful people and to pour out His blood as the ransom price for sinners everywhere. When Jesus ascended back to heaven, He made His way into the holy of holies in the heavenly tabernacle of God to pour out that blood upon the altar as an everlasting atonement for anyone who would believe on Him. "For Christ has not entered into the holy places made with hands, which are copies of the true; but into heaven itself, now to appear in the presence of God for us" (Heb 9:24).

The evidence seems to indicate that the great work of Christ was not His life, but His death. He was born miraculously. He lived victoriously. He died vicariously. He arose triumphantly. He ascended gloriously. The Gospels give a prominence to the closing scenes of His life. His blood atonement seems to command a place of priority in the Scriptures.

The ordinances of the church point to His atoning death. Baptism does not symbolize His mighty miracles or His penetrating sermons. In baptism the believer is "baptized into his death" and "buried with Him through baptism into death" (Rm 6:3-4). The Lord's Supper does not commemorate the excellent example He set forth in His daily life. It points to His death. The elements of the Lord's Supper are reminders of the broken body and shed blood of Jesus on Calvary's cross.

The believer cannot make too much of the rich, red, royal blood of Jesus Christ. D. L. Moody was preaching on the precious blood of Jesus one evening as he frequently did. After the sermon a critic accosted Moody and curtly commented, "Mr. Moody, I disliked your sermon; and I disagreed with it." The bold, but unlettered evangelist said, "Well, Sir, what was there about my sermon with which you so strongly disagreed?"

The man, who was a preacher himself, said, "Mr. Moody, you are always preaching about the blood of Jesus. Why do you preach such a gory and grotesque gospel?" He continued, "I don't ever preach about the blood or the cross. I preach on other subjects."

Mr. Moody said, "Well, what do you do with 1 Peter 1:18-19, 'Knowing that you were not redeemed with corruptible things, *like* silver or gold, from your aimless conduct received by tradition from your fathers, but with the precious blood of Christ, as of a lamb without blemish and without spot.'"

The man said, "Well, I just wouldn't use that kind of Scripture passage in any of my sermons."

Moody said, "What do you do with Hebrews 9:22: 'And according to the law almost all things are purified with blood, and without shedding of blood there is not remission.'?"

The man said, "I just don't preach on that verse."

Moody inquired, "What do you do with Colossians 1:14: 'In whom we have redemption through his blood, the forgiveness of sin'?"

The man said, "I just don't preach sermons on the blood."

Mr. Moody, who was zealous for the truth of God, said, "Good heavens, Man! You're not preaching the gospel! You're lecturing moral essays."

The gospel of Jesus Christ is the gospel of blood redemption. This is the theme that runs throughout the Word of God. There is a red river of redemption that flows from the gates of the Garden of Eden all the way to the blood-bought saints of God who stand around the throne in celebrative worship.

From the very first pages of Genesis, the Word teaches that Cain's offering was not acceptable to God because there was no blood in it. God's prescription from the very beginning was that there should be a blood sacrifice to atone for sins. Cain brought vegetables, the work of his own hands. Perhaps that is where we got our phrase, "You can't get blood out of a turnip."

The Bible declares that Abel brought of the firstling of his flock and of the fat thereof and the Lord had respect unto Abel and to his offering. The writer of Hebrews said. "By faith Abel offered to God a more excellent sacrifice than Cain" (11:4). So, the blood sacrifice of Jesus shed on Calvary's cross and poured out in heaven's holy of holies brings to a glorious crescendo the anthem of blood redemption that is pictured on every page in the Word of God.

6. The Sanctuary of This Priesthood

The exalted position from which our High Priest now operates is "at the right hand of the throne of the Majesty in the heavens" (Heb 8:1). This heavenly throne room is the sanctuary made not by man, but by God Himself. This lofty position signifies that Jesus Christ is a royal High Priest with a lordship that is unrivaled.

He is also described as a minister of the sanctuary. The word for minister is *leitourgos*. This word is used to describe a public servant, a minister. In Christ lies the rare combination of supreme majesty and supreme service. Even from His throne on high, He condescends to minister to us in His compassion and intercession.

In His last message to the church, Jesus said, "To him who overcomes will I grant to sit with Me on My Throne, as I also overcame and sat down with My Father on His throne" (Rv 3:21). How did Jesus earn the privilege to sit on the heavenly throne at His Father's right hand? As the second person in the Godhead, He had a perfect right to sit there, but remember also that He humbled Himself and took upon Himself the form of man and became obedient unto death. By His life of service and sacrifice He has been given an exalted position in glory. He said, "Therefore My Father loves Me, because I lay down My life that I might take it again. No one takes it from Me, but I lay it down of Myself. I have power to lay it down, and I have power to take it again. This command have I received of my Father" (Jn 10:17-18).

In an unusual way Jesus sensed the Father's love because of His obedience unto death. Jesus said, "A disciple is not above his teacher, nor a servant above his Master" (Mt 10:24). The footprints of Jesus are our guide. If we follow in the steps of Jesus, if we minister as He ministered, if we obey as He obeyed, if we suffer as He suffered, one day we will reign with Him. Salvation is free, but genuine priesthood, which is more than just a title, is earned at a tremendous price.

Notes

1. Hardin Craig, *Shakespeare* (Chicago: Scott, Foresman and Company, 1958), p. 929.

2. Quoted in Arthur W. Pink, *An Exposition of Hebrews* (Grand Rapids: Baker Book House, 1954), p. 422.

5

Entering into the Holiest (Matthew 27:50-51)

Within every man there is a God-shaped vacuum. A study of anthropology reveals that enthroned in every man's heart is a god whom he worships. Even among aboriginal tribes in the remote comers of the earth there are rites of worship.

Undoubtedly, the god revered by many is a false god; nevertheless, every man worships something or someone. Oftentimes when man dethrones God, he deifies himself. Only the fool says, "There is no god" (Ps 14:1). However, those who know the true and living God desire fellowship with Him. The child of God wants to enter into the presence of the Heavenly Father. The psalmist said, "As the deer pants for the water brooks, so pants my soul for You, O God" (Ps 42:1). David declared, "O God, You are my God; early will I seek You; my soul thirsts for You; my flesh longs for You in a dry and thirsty land, where there is no water" (Ps 63:1). Paul expressed a desire for an intimate fellowship with the Lord (Phil 3:10).

The first man of creation had personal access to the majesty of God. Before the forbidden tree had yielded its fateful fruit and before the tempter had touched the world, Adam had the joyful experience of entering into the presence of the Lord and fellowshipping with Him on an intimate basis.

Both Adam and Eve had apparently come to enjoy a close, personal relationship with God. It was not uncustomary for God to walk about the Garden of Eden in the cool of the day. That first couple recognized the very voice of God. They rejoiced in every opportunity to commune with Him.

When by disobedience sin entered into the world, everything changed. After trespassing the command of God, Adam and Eve hid themselves from His presence. Consequently, the Lord God, who cannot even bear to look upon sin, bolted the door of access into the glory of His presence. We know that God placed cherubim with a flaming sword on the east side of the Garden of Eden to keep Adam and all succeeding generations from the tree of life.

Interestingly, the Bible always associates the cherubim with the throne of God. The Scriptures avow that the Lord reigns and sits between the cherubim (Ps 99:1). Since cherubim were sent to guard "the way of the tree of life" (Gn 3:24) in the Garden of Eden, we may conclude that is where God's presence was especially manifested in that day.

When the Temple was constructed, the presence of the Lord was specifically revealed in the holy of holies above the mercy seat. Once again, the emblematic cherubim were constructed to overshadow the mercy seat. They were embroidered upon a special veil which was made to conceal the glory of God.

I. THE VEIL IS REMARKABLE

Special consideration must be given to the veil because it is essential to a proper understanding of the doctrine of the priesthood of the believer. The veil concealed the glory of God. The rending of the veil at the death of Christ symbolizes the opening of the way of access into the throne of God. Indeed, the veil which essentially represents the flesh of

Christ, is in itself remarkable in its construction, its obstruction, and its instruction.

1. The Veil Is Remarkable in Its Construction

God gave to Moses specific instructions concerning the construction of the tabernacle (Ex 26-27). The tabernacle was to be placed in the center of the twelve tribes of Israel with three tribes camping on each side. This specially designed tent was to be located within a courtyard, fenced about with fine twined linen (Ex 27:9).

The tabernacle consisted primarily of two rooms. The outer room containing the table of shewbread, the candlestick, and the altar of incense was called the holy place. The inner room containing the ark of the covenant and the dwelling place of God was the holy of holies. Separating the holy place from the holy of holies was a curtain or a veil, "You shall hang the veil from the clasps ... and the veil shall be a divider between the holy place and the Most Holy" (26:33). This curtain served to veil the presence of God from those who ministered in the holy place.

The construction of the veil is fascinating and most arresting because of its symbolism. God specified to Moses: "You shall make a veil woven of blue, purple, and scarlet thread" (26:31). One must remember that the veil is representative of the Lord Jesus Christ.

The colors are also beautifully emblematic. Blue is the first color mentioned. God has chosen to paint the vast expanse of the heavens in shades of blue. As "the heavens declare the glory of God" (Ps 19:1), the blue declares that Jesus came down from heaven as the Son of God. This color speaks of the divinity of Christ.

The scarlet speaks of the humanity of Christ. As the blue speaks of the hues of the heavens, the red speaks of earth tones. I can attest to this because my first home was in the red clay hills of North Carolina. A number of years ago, on a family vacation in the western part of the country, we visited Sedona, Arizona. The colorful rock formations that lined the highway were magnificent. As the sun set every shade of red imaginable could be seen in the sandstone skyscrapers that graced the horizon.

The color of the earth in Palestine to which Christ came has tints of red. As a heavenward glance produces vistas of blue, an earthward glance provides remnants of red. Interestingly, the name of the first man of creation, Adam, means "red," or "from the earth." Jesus, the second Adam, was clothed in the humanity of the first Adam.

Furthermore, red and blood are often thought of almost synonymously. Jesus had to take upon Himself our humanity. He had to take upon himself the likeness of man in order to shed His blood and die the death that would redeem man from sin and guilt.

A proper mixture of blue and red produces purple. The purple speaks of the perfect blend of Christ's divinity and humanity. The intermingling of the blue of Christ's divinity and the red of His humanity produces the unique God-man, who is perfectly qualified to be the "Mediator between God and men" (1 Tm 2:5).

The purple also signifies the royalty of Christ. Before His crucifixion, the Roman soldiers ridiculed Jesus by clothing Him with a purple robe and crowning Him with a crown of thorns (Mk 15:17). Even though those soldiers saluted Jesus in mockery, they unknowingly previewed the day when all men will bow before Him as the "Lord of lords and the King of kings."

Notice that the veil was made of "fine woven linen" (Ex 26:31,36). This material speaks of the moral excellency of the Lord Jesus. It affirms that there is no coarseness in His character and no blemish in His life. The Scripture states that "fine linen is the righteous acts of saints" (Rv 19:8). Since God has made Jesus to be to every believer "righteousness, and sanctification, and redemption" (1 Cor1:30), the fine twined linen seems to portray "the righteous one."

God specified to Moses that the veil was to be made "of cunning work." Even as this curtain before the holy of holies was beautifully designed and skillfully wrought, so was the incarnation of Christ. It took the omniscience of God to design for Christ a human nature that was without sin. The Bible attests to the wonder of Christ's birth (Lk 1:35) and the uniqueness of His human nature (Heb 10:5). It was "a cunning work."

Additionally, the Lord instructed that cherubim should be embroidered on the veil. The emblematic presence of these angelic beings gave added emphasis to the reality that no man could gain access beyond the veil. When Adam and Eve were expelled from their earthly paradise the cherubim with the flaming sword guarded the entrance to the Garden of Eden. Similarly, the cherubim stitched in mystic form upon the veil suggested a heavenly watch-care over the majesty of God within the holy of holies. The unrent veil and the embroidered cherubim combined to enforce the reality of "no access" into the presence of God.

2. The Veil Is Remarkable in Its Obstruction

The ark of the covenant and the mercy seat were located behind the veil. The sacred desk known as the ark of the covenant or the ark of testimony was made out of acacia wood and inlaid with gold. The mercy seat was a covering of pure gold placed on top of the ark. The ark of the covenant and the mercy seat were fitted together and combined to make the only piece of furniture in the holy of holies. Upon the mercy seat the Lord dwelt in His Shechinah glory. He declared, "I will appear in the cloud above the mercy seat" (Lv 16:2). When Moses went into the tabernacle, he heard the Lord "speaking unto him from above the mercy seat that was on the ark of testimony" (Nm 7:89).

Only one man among all the Israelites could ever enter into the holy of holies: the high priest. Only one day out of the entire year could the high priest enter into the holy of holies: The Day of Atonement. The high priest could enter the holy of holies on that one day only on the basis of shed blood. Only by the blood of an animal slain as a sacrifice for sin could the high priest fold back the veil and enter into God's dwelling place. This Old Testament mediator sprinkled the blood of the sin offering seven times upon the mercy seat on the Day of Atonement. Based upon these stringent conditions, the high priest could enter the holy of holies and commune with God on behalf of the people.

Any violation of this divinely prescribed arrangement for entering within the veil meant certain death. "The Lord said to Moses: 'Tell Aaron your brother not to come at just any time into the Holy Place inside the veil, before the mercy seat which is on the ark; lest he die" (Lv 16:2). The instantaneous death of Nadab and Abihu perfectly illustrates that God will keep His word concerning those who disobey His instructions and ordinances.

Consequently, the veil was remarkable in its obstruction. It vehemently cried out, "No trespassing!" The purpose of the veil was not to provide a way to God. The purpose of the veil was to conceal the Shechinah glory of the Lord and bar the way of access into His presence.

3. The Veil Is Remarkable in Its Instruction

The veil teaches that we are not saved by the life of Jesus, but by His death. The colorful and cunningly crafted curtain before the holy of holies typifies the body of Christ. In His body Jesus lived a beautiful, sinless life. He was the epitome of goodness. In His life is the fruit of the Spirit in all of its manifestations. Jesus never lost His temper. He never said a thoughtless word. He never had an impure thought. He never did an unkind deed. He never even had an evil inclination. In fact, He was anointed with the Holy Spirit and with power and "went about doing good" (Ac 10:38). He healed the sick, raised the dead, loved the unlovely, gave to the poor, set the captives free, and spent time with children. His earthly life, like the veil in the tabernacle, was compellingly attractive and appealing.

The lifestyle of Jesus is forever an indictment against human sinfulness. Everyone's effort to emulate the example of Christ falls pitifully short of the pattern He established. In the middle ages, Thomas a Kempis wrote a simple, little book called *The Imitation of Christ*. The book sets forth a noble concept but those who expect to find eternal life by imitating the life of Christ are going to find that it is an impossible dream.

In a more recent classic, *In His Steps*, by Charles M. Sheldon, the author asked, "What would Jesus do?" It is a good question to ask, but for centuries men have discovered that they have neither the grace nor the power to react in every circumstance as Jesus would.

The rich, young ruler saw the perfection of Jesus and called Him "Good Teacher." Then he asked, "What good thing shall I do that I may have eternal life?" (Mt 19:16). Jesus said, "If you want to be perfect, go, sell what you have and give to the poor, and you will have treasure in heaven: and come, follow Me" (v. 21). Jesus helped this young man who thought he had kept all the commandments to see the glaring deficiencies in his life. The youthful inquirer departed sorrowfully because he realized that he could never be good ("perfect") like the "Good Teacher."

Yet is it not by the extraordinary life of Jesus that we gain access into the presence of God? In fact, those who are trusting in the life of Jesus to redeem them are crushed upon the very rock in which they are trusting. No man can effectively emulate the example of Jesus. Therefore, salvation is neither in the perfection of Christ's life nor earned in man's attempt at that perfection.

The instruction received from the unrent veil is beautiful. As perfectly as the veil was constructed, it was positioned before the holy of holies not for ornamentation, but to prevent access into the presence of God. Only as the veil was rent, representing the rending and breaking of the body of Jesus on the cross, would the true way to God be made accessible.

II. THE VEIL IS RENT

Exodus 40 gives a record of how the tabernacle was erected. All of the furniture, the taches, the boards, the bars, the pillars, the sockets, the candlesticks, the coverings, and the curtains were completed. The Scripture relates that Moses himself "finished the work" (Ex 40:33). God inspected the work and displayed His pleasure by filling the holy of holies with His glory. The veil hung before the ark of the covenant throughout all the days of the tabernacle to conceal the *Shechinah* glory of God.

After almost five hundred years, the tabernacle was replaced by Solomon's Temple; but the veil of the Temple was the veil of the tabernacle perpetuated. The latter veil was a reproduction of the former, but it served the exact same purpose. It was hung as a covering of concealment before the ark of the covenant. For centuries in the tabernacle and then in the Temple, the veil was positioned to shield the presence of God. However, on the day Christ died, after almost fifteen hundred years of hiding the glory of God, the veil was rent asunder. "Then, behold, the veil of the temple was torn in two from top to bottom; and the earth quaked, and the rocks were split" (Mt 27:51).

1. When Was the Veil Rent?

The veil in the Temple was torn apart the very moment Christ died on the cross. While suspended between heaven and earth on a cruel cross, Jesus died as the Savior of the world. In the instant of His death, the veil held by the "golden hooks" from above was rent.

On the day Christ died, an uncanny darkness engulfed the earth at high noon (Lk 23:44). For three hours the daystar wore a black shroud of mourning. When the sun dared to cast her rays of light upon the earth again, the three crosses on that barren skull-shaped hill appeared only as silhouettes. As the darkness diminished and the light increased, the God-man on the middle cross was heard to cry again with a loud voice. With a shout of victory, He "yielded up His spirit" (Mt 27:50). Concurrently with His death the veil was rent in the Temple. God designed that it should be so.

Years ago, an astronomer came to the personal realization that God had created a universe that was absolutely precise in its order and movement. He learned through his studies that the timing of the alignment of certain heavenly bodies could be calculated with pinpoint accuracy. He told His assistant that his computations indicated that a certain alignment in the heavens would occur at an appointed time. His calculations were down to the very second. His assistant was instructed to keep his eye on the second hand of the clock that hung on the wall.

At the specified time, he was to hit the table with a mallet. As the astronomer looked through the telescope in the observatory, he indicated that when the precise alignment occurred, he would say, "Now!" After a long wait the silence of the observatory was interrupted when the astronomer said, "Now!" and the assistant's mallet hit the table simultaneously.

In the very same way, God arranged the death of Jesus and the rending of the veil concurrently. In the very moment Mary witnessed the dying breath of Jesus, the priest who was ministering in the holy place viewed in stunned disbelief the rending of the veil. Thus, we know when it was rent.

2. By Whom Was It Rent?

Some people attribute the rending of the veil to the earthquake which occurred on the afternoon of Christ's death. It seems unreasonable to suppose that an earthquake could tear asunder a loose hanging curtain without shaking to pieces the Temple where the veil hung. It is more sensible to conclude that both the earthquake and the tearing of the veil were concurrent consequences of the cry of Jesus (Mt 27:50-51).

That the veil was torn thoroughly from the top to the bottom is quite a miracle in light of all the evidence considered. Speculations have been offered that the veil was as much as four inches thick or at least as thick as the width of a man's hand. Tradition has supported the belief that two teams of oxen pulling against each other, as in a tug of war, could not have torn the veil apart.

The key to understanding the cause of the rent is the evangelist's report that it was torn, not from the bottom to the top, but "from top to bottom" (Mt 27:51). This indicates that the veil was torn by the same One who smote the suffering substitute on the cross. The Bible says that the Messiah was "smitten by God" (Is 53:4) and that "yet it pleased the Lord [Jehovah] to bruise him" (v.10). The religious leaders instigated Jesus' death. Pontius Pilate permitted His death. The Roman soldiers implemented His death. However, God was ultimately responsible for the death of His Son. In Christianity God, not man, provides the sacrifice. "For God so loved the world that He gave His only begotten Son" (Jn 3:16).

3. Where Was It Rent?

"The veil of the temple was torn in two from top to bottom" (Mt 27:51). Not one thread in the breach was left intact. The tear in the curtain was complete. Even so the atoning work of Christ was finished. There is nothing man can do or needs to do to supplement the dying of the Savior on Calvary's tree.

> Not by works of righteousness which we have done, but according to His mercy He saved us, through the washing of regeneration and renewing of the Holy Spirit, whom He poured out on us abundantly through Jesus Christ our Saviour (Ti 3:5-6).

Occasionally people will try to establish certain do-it-yourself, or self-help, projects to get to God. The projects are what might be called "religious." They stand in striking contrast to Christianity, whereby God offers the avenue of approach.

For example, consider the contrast between Babel and Bethlehem. At Babel the people said, "Come, let us build ourselves a city, and a tower whose top is in the heavens" (Gn 11:4). Babel's tower of blunders is an everlasting reminder of man's incapacity to approach God through self-effort. Conversely, Bethlehem offers the beautiful picture of God reaching down to man in unfeigned love and providing the means of ultimate access into His presence.

Where was the veil rent? It was rent not only completely from the top to the bottom but also "in the midst" (Lk 23:45, KJV). This rending of the veil indicates that the ark of the covenant and the mercy seat were fully exposed. There was now a way of direct access with no detours into the presence of God through the Son.

4. Why Was It Rent?

The veil in the Temple was rent so that the instrument of separation might become an open thoroughfare for sinners to God. Have you ever been denied entrance into a place where you wanted to gain access? Have you ever then known the joy of admission into the place from which you were formerly excluded?

In the spring of 2020, the world experienced a virtual lockdown because of the Coronavirus (COVID-19) pandemic. The United States was severely impacted by the rampaging illness. Our granddaughter, Grace Harris, who worked for the New York Metropolitan Baptist Association, was living in the epicenter of the pandemic. My wife, Martha Jean, and I were naturally concerned about her, but there was no way we could get to see her. Senior adults were urged by Georgia Governor Brian Kemp to remain at home. New York Governor Andrew Cuomo ordered a statewide lockdown as the crisis spiraled out of control in the Empire State. Flights to New York City were being cancelled. Strict measures including social distancing, home-sheltering and quarantines were mandated. Imagine my joy when the quarantine was lifted, and I was privileged to visit Grace and all my grandchildren. It is generally true that there is a tragedy about exclusion and a triumph about inclusion.

This torn curtain brought to an end an era of exclusion. The Old Testament dispensation of the Levitical priesthood was now history. The rending of the veil meant that the middle wall of partition between Jews and Gentiles was removed. This cataclysmic event opened the way for every believer to be his own priest unto God.

III. THE VEIL IS REMOVED

For all intents and purposes the veil ceased to exist after the death of Jesus. The concealment of the holy of holies came to an end. Today nothing prevents the believers from being "partakers of the inheritance of the saints" (Col 1:12), and believers have every reason and motive to draw near unto God. "But now in Christ Jesus you who were once far off have been brought near by the blood of Christ. For He Himself is our peace, who has made both one, and has broken down the middle wall of separation" (Eph 2:13-14). Because Christ received the penalty of sin deserved by us, we may enter into the reward deserved by Him.

A passage beautifully illustrating the inheritance of the believer-priest is Hebrews 10:19-22:

> Therefore, brethren, having boldness to enter the Holiest by the blood of Jesus, by a new and living way which He conse-crated for us, through the veil, that is, His flesh, and *having* a High Priest over the house of God, let us draw near with a true heart in full assurance of faith, having our hearts sprin-kled from an evil conscience and our bodies washed with pure water.

The removal of the veil of concealment beautifully portrays for the believer-priest the way of approach to God. Let us consider the way and the worship of the believer-priest.

1. The Way of the Believer-Priest

According to Hebrews 10:20, the avenue of approach into the holiest is "by a new and living way." The word "new" is the translation of a Greek word that occurs only this one time in the New Testament. The Greek word is *prosphatos*, originally meaning "freshly slaughtered." Jesus, the freshly slaughtered sacrifice, opens up the way of access to God.

The way of the old covenant was the way of death. The only way God could be approached under the Levitical priesthood was through the death of an animal. Christ, the "living way," is the avenue of approach in the new priestly order. Every believer is a priest unto God with free access to the throne of the Heavenly Father through the Son.

Furthermore, the believer may "enter into the holiest" with boldness. When the veil was rent, it required some real courage for the priests within the tabernacle to gaze upon the mercy seat. For them to have fled in fear of sudden death would not have been surprising. Neverthe-less, today the Holy Spirit invites the believer not only to look at the holy of holies but also to enter into God's presence with confidence.

One need never draw near to God with fear and trepidation because every believer can have the assurance of God's love and of this gift of His only begotten Son for the redemption of all who would believe. Since Calvary the believer is accepted "in the beloved" (Eph 1:6). The Greek word for "boldness" is *parrhesia* which comes from *pas* meaning "all" and *rhesis* meaning "speech." The word denotes "a boldness to speak" or a "spirit of courage."

The same Greek word is used several times in the Epistle to the He-brews. Apparently, the Hebrew Christians were tempted to be timo-rous, with a propensity toward quitting or giving up on Christ. Too often people approach God with an unholy reticence. Believers sheep-ishly draw near to God to make their petition. Worship is unenthusi-astically offered. Love is hesitatingly expressed. The approach to God is often apologetic and reluctant or perhaps like a burglar or an intruder entering a house.

Believers forget that they have been made "a kingdom of priests" unto God and that high privileges come with the office of priest. There is spiritual business to be conducted in the presence of the Heavenly Father and the believer-priest is to enter into the holy place with confi-dence to fulfill his mission.

The apostle Paul testified to his boldness before God in his Epistle to the Ephesians. He said, "We have boldness and access with confidence through faith in Him" (Eph 3:12). Having boldly entered into the pres-ence of God, the great apostle could fearlessly stand before men. To the people of Thessalonica, he could say, "We were bold in our God to speak to you the gospel of God with much conflict" (1 Thes 2:2).

In Antioch, Paul and Barnabas reportedly "grew bold" (Ac 13:46). In Ephesus, Paul "went into the synagogue and spoke boldly for three months, reasoning and persuading concerning the things of the king-dom of God" (Ac 19:8). Paul's boldness before God gave him the ability to speak courageously for Christ in any situation. The way of the be-

liever-priest into the presence of God is the "new and living way" provided by the death of Christ.

Sometimes doctrinal studies on the priesthood of believers stop at
this point. The spotlight is cast upon the privilege of entering into the
holiest. Nowhere does biblical theology emphasize privilege without responsibility. Being given the rich inheritance of priesthood does not
mean that the believer can run in and out of God's presence indiscreetly
or casually. Priesthood does not give the believer the liberty to claim
infallibility concerning which portion of Scripture is true and which
portion is errant. As a believer-priest one does not have the privilege of
devising one's own method of approach in worship. As a believer-priest
the saint of God is an heir of the Heavenly Father and a joint heir of
Jesus Christ. However, being a priest does not qualify the believer for
the Godhead. The New Testament priest remains forever the offeror of
worship and not the object of worship.

2. The Worship of the Believer-Priest

Once the way is opened by the sacrifice of Christ, what is the believer-priest to do with the privilege of "entering into the holiest?" He is
to combine responsibility with privilege and worship the Lord in a way
that is acceptable to Him. What kind of worship can the believer-priest
offer that will be received by the Heavenly Father? Listen to Romans
12:1: "I beseech you therefore, brethren, by the mercies of God, that you
present your bodies a living sacrifice, holy, acceptable to God, which is
your reasonable service [worship]."

The priests of the Old Testament were always associated with the
element of sacrifice. The priest of Melchizedek's order was known for
his sacrifice. The New Testament Christian who desires to add authenticity to the new priestly order will be known for his sacrifice. There
is a sense in which the child of God should present his body as a living sacrifice every day. The death-to-self principle is admonished in the
Word of God. Daily, as the believer denies self, reckons self dead, and

comes alive unto God, one's life, worship, and service are acceptable to the Heavenly Father.

Let the believer never forget that the way of access has been provided that "[we might] draw near with a true heart in full assurance of faith" (Heb 10:22). Having drawn near, the believer is to present his body as a "living sacrifice" (Rm 12:1). Incidentally, God never accepts the offering in part; He only accepts the whole. That body is to be totally God's. The offering must be all or nothing. He is Lord of all or not Lord at all. God wants every believer-priest to be wholly, totally offered to Him as a living sacrifice.

There is a wealth of meaning in the phrase "living sacrifice." The word "living" has its roots in the sacrifices of the Old Testament. The reference is to a sacrifice that is placed upon the altar forever. When the Levitical priest brought that offering, he remained at the altar with utensils known as flesh hooks. With these utensils the priest continually brought the sacrifice back to the center of the flame upon the brazen altar until the offering was totally consumed. The responsible believer-priest knows little about true significance of "entering into the holiest" until he has totally surrendered his life to God and placed it upon the altar of sacrifice until it is totally consumed.

I once knew a man whose life was obviously on the altar of sacrifice. His name was Charlie Compton. I met him at a Royal Ambassador Camp in Fruitland, North Caroling when I was a young teenager, but he greatly impacted my life in the course of that one week, because his life was conspicuously one of surrender and his messages were so clearly anointed by the Holy Spirit.

He had played football at the University of Alabama and was known as "the man of steel." I think he would have been a first-round draft pick in the National Football League, but his football career at Alabama was interrupted by World War II. As a patriot he went off to fight in the war and became a highly decorated war hero. When he returned from the war, he completed his education at Alabama and began preparing for missionary service. As a student athlete he taught Sunday School at the Baptist Student Center, spoke at the Tuscaloosa jail on Sunday Af-

ternoon, and preached in a church somewhere in Alabama on Sunday
night.

Charlie Compton married Betsy Dunning on June 19, 1948, less than
two weeks after graduating from the University of Alabama. According
to Wayne Atcheson, the author of *Fifty Years of Crimson Tide Faith*, Charlie went to Southwestern Baptist Theological Seminary in Fort Worth,
Texas, to prepare for missionary service and upon graduation told the
Foreign Mission Board (now the International Mission Board) that he
wanted to go where no other missionary wanted to go. He got his destination wish and went to a place called Mato Grosso in Brazil. Atcheson writes, "The area was larger than Texas . . . There were 16 churches
when he arrived and 215 when his sudden and untimely death occurred
in 1972 as the result of an automobile accident in Brazil."[1]

Compton made such an impact upon his alma mater, his nation and
the cause of Christ that since 1960 the University of Alabama football
team has a Squad Sunday every August at Calvary Baptist Church in
Tuscaloosa and selects a winner of the *Christian Example Award* known
as the *Charlie Compton Award*. Atcheson summarizes Compton's life
with these words,

> The story of Charlie Compton is heart wrenching, spe-
> cialty the way he served with a sold-out passion to
> Almighty God to people he may have only seen but one
> time.
>
> We'll probably never see the likes of a Charlie Compton
> again, but his life and mission rank him as one of the greatest
> Christians we'll every know or read about. He literally gave his
> life to Jesus Christ on the mission field. He was 49 years old
> (when he died) and will always be an unforgettable inspira-
> tion.[2]

Once Charlie Compton understood that the wall of partition between him and God had been removed, once he came to understand his
calling, he was consumed upon the altar of surrender and sacrifice.

Notes

[1]Wayne Atcheson, *Fifty Years of Crimson Tide Faith* (Waxlaw: Influence Press, 2014), pp. 282-283.

[2]Ibid.

6

The Priest and His Portable Temple (1 Peter 2:5)

A physical structure of brick, mortar, steel, and glass cannot identify the true church. Neither can the chasuble, stole, miter, and alb worn as vestments in some ecclesiastical orders identify the New Testament priesthood. The visible church on earth is not denoted by Gothic, Romanesque, Renaissance, Colonial, or modem architectural design, but by those people whose lives have been changed by the power of God. The new priestly order cannot be discerned by singling out only those people who preside over the Eucharist, conduct mass, and preach from ornate pulpits.

Ever since that first Good Friday when Christ was crucified, there has been no need for a select group of priests. Every believer has become a part of that "holy priesthood." In Revelation 1:6, the apostle John said, He "has made us kings and priests to his God and Father." The "us" in that passage of Scripture includes all those who have been redeemed by the blood of Calvary.

Peter wrote in his first epistle: "You also, as living stones, are being built up a spiritual house, an holy priesthood, to offer up spiritual sacrifices acceptable to God through Christ Jesus" (1 Pt 2:5). In this text three notable things are evident. The apostle Peter wrote of the matter of a spiritual edifice, a spiritual office, and spiritual sacrifice.

I. A SPIRITUAL EDIFICE

In 1 Peter 2:5 the believers are described as "living stones...being built up [into] a spiritual house." This speaks of the church of the living God as a building. In the New Testament the church is described as the body of Christ (Eph 1:22-23), the bride of Christ (Eph 5:22-32), and the building of Christ (1 Cor 3:9).

When the church is referred to as a spiritual building, Christ is regarded as the chief cornerstone. This strategic position in the building of this spiritual edifice was foreordained by God. Years before the incarnation God said, "Behold, I lay in Zion a stone for a foundation, a tried stone, a precious cornerstone, a sure foundation" (Is 28:16). Those who have put their faith and trust in this stone have found Him to be precious (1 Pt 2:7).

Having trusted in Christ, the believer becomes an integral part of His body. Paul said of this spiritual edifice in Ephesians 2:20-21 that it is "built on the foundation of the apostles and prophets, Jesus Christ Himself being the chief cornerstone in whom the whole building being fitted together, grows unto a holy temple in the Lord." The reference here is to the true church, the eternal church, made up of every kindred, tongue and nation that one day the Lord will present to Himself as glorious "not having spot, or wrinkle, or any such thing" (Eph 5:27).

When Peter spoke of the believer as a "living stone," he was surely reflecting upon a personal experience that he once had with Christ. Years before at Caesarea Philippi, Jesus had posed a question to His disciples: "But who do you say that I am?" Peter was the first to respond, "You are the Christ, the Son of the living God" (Mt 16:16). Upon hearing Peter's confession, Jesus said, "Blessed are you, Simon Bar-Jonah: for flesh and blood has not revealed this to you, but My Father who is in heaven. And I also say to you that you are Peter [*Petros*], and on this rock [*pe-*

tra] I will build My church" (vv. 17-18). *Petros* is a rock or a stone which might be placed into the wall of a building. This word is not the designated term for the foundation or the base upon which the building stands. The word for foundation is *petra*. *Petra* is a cognate word related to the root word *petros*, but it is a different word entirely. *Petra* speaks of a ledge or a cliff of rock, like that in Matthew 7:24 upon which the wise man built his house. *Petros* is a piece of rock, but *petra* is the foundation stone, the essential rock. Jesus declared that Peter would be one of the building blocks for the raising of this spiritual edifice called the church. Peter, in a reminiscent mood, declared that every believer has become a living stone for this "spiritual house" that someday will be completed.

Consider also that every believer, although a part of the whole, is a microcosm of the whole. The child of God is a picture of the "spiritual house" in miniature, for every believer has become the temple of God. Paul asked, " Do you not know that your body is the temple of the Holy Spirit who is in you, whom you have from God, and you are not your own?" (1 Cor 6:19). That the Holy Spirit should condescend to indwell humankind is an utter amazement, but it is a reality. "But. if the Spirit of Him who raised Jesus from the dead dwells in you, He who raised up Christ from the dead will also give life to your mortal bodies through his Spirit that dwells in you" (Rm 8:11). Every believer has become a spiritual edifice with a royal resident, as well as a building block in God's eternal church.

Throughout history God has occupied many houses; however, God cannot abide in a defiled and desecrated house. Therefore, God vacates any dwelling that becomes polluted or unclean.

Consider the four houses in which God has lived. God's primary house was a man named Adam. The Bible says, "And the Lord God formed man of the dust of the ground, and breathed into his nostrils the breath of life; and man became a living being" (Gn 2:7). This Scripture highlights the triune nature of man: body, spirit, and soul. So, the first dwelling place of God was designed by Him to reflect His triunity. Tragically, Adam fell through disobedience and entertained sin in the house that was designed to entertain God. Consequently, God moved

out of His primary house and that house was destroyed. God had said,
"... in the day that you eat [of the forbidden fruit] you shall surely die"
(v. 17).

God's second dwelling was His pattern house, the Temple. Solomon
said, "I have surely built You an exalted house and a place for You to
dwell in" (1 Kgs 8:13). Both the tabernacle and the Temple were "copies
of the things in the heavens" (Heb 9:23; also see 8:5). The holy of holies,
the inner sanctum of the Temple, was the dwelling place of the Shechinah glory of God. God's pattern house was His place of residency for
many years. Once again, the house of God was desecrated. Jesus referred
to the Temple when He said, "My house shall be called a house of prayer,
but you have made it 'a den of thieves' " (Mt 21:13). The Lord then declared as translated in the *King James Version*, "Behold, your house is
left to you desolate" (23:38). The defilement of the Temple changed the
possessive pronoun from "My" to "your." Sin's entrance into the Temple necessitated God's exit. In AD 70, Titus and his marching Roman
hordes came into Jerusalem and destroyed the city, including the Temple, God's pattern house.

The third dwelling in which God chose to take up residency was His
perfect house, the Lord Jesus Christ Himself. Jesus speaks of His body as
a temple in John 2:19-21. In John 1:14, the Apostle John wrote, "And the
Word became flesh, and dwelt among us." In Jesus, God clothed Himself in human flesh and tabernacled among men. Then, astonishingly,
God's perfect house was desecrated. Jesus did not defile Himself in any
way, for He was sinless; however, the Bible says, "For He made Him who
knew no sin to be sin for us, that we might become the righteousness of
God in Him" (2 Cor 5:21). The sins of the whole world were placed upon
that perfect house and it was polluted. Once again God exited when sin
entered. The exit of God prompted Jesus to cry from Calvary, "My God,
my God, why have You forsaken me?" (Mt 27:46).

God's primary house was for fellowship. God's pattern house was for
instruction. God's perfect house was for redemption. However, God's
great desire was to find a permanent house. He has found that permanent dwelling within every believer. There is a marvelous mystery

about the incarnation. That God inhabited the babe in Bethlehem is an astounding wonder. The marvel of all marvels, however, is that God would inhabit the sons of men and indwell forever all who believe on Him. Jesus said, "And I will pray the Father, and He will give you another Helper, that He may abide with you forever" (Jn 14:16) The Apostle Paul underscored the words of Jesus when he stated that believers are sealed with the Holy Spirit of promise until the day of redemption (see Eph 1: 12-14). Every believer is a spiritual edifice with a royal resident.

II. A SPIRITUAL OFFICE

Peter wrote, "You also, as living stones, are being built up a spiritual house, an holy priesthood" (1 Pt 2:5). In continuing his emphasis upon this spiritual office, Peter called it "a royal priesthood" (v. 9). "Holy priesthood" denotes a spiritual office. Those priests fulfilling this office have the responsibility of offering sacrifices acceptable to God. "Royal priesthood" is a term which pertains to the royal dignity of showing forth the majesty of the Lord.

1. The Sacredness of the Spiritual Office

This priesthood of which Peter wrote is sacred, "holy." Today, as in the past, many religions have priests. There are also many perversions of the priesthood within Christianity. New Testament priesthood, however, is not fundamentally materialistic, ritualistic, or humanistic. It is spiritual and demands holiness.

Charles Haddon Spurgeon wrote:

> I think I see the world's priests, decorated with divers robes and ornaments; a gallant show, indeed, for fools to stare at. I see them with their colors various, with their shaven heads or unshaven, as the case may be! These be the priests of Baal: mere mimics, servants of the visible

shrine, servitors of idols; these be not the priests of the living God, who is a spirit, and is served by spiritual priests.[1]

The new priestly order existent under Christ's headship is meant to be holy. There is a sacredness about this spiritual office.

Many believer-priests today are going down like tenpins because they have not maintained the standard of holiness. Many of God's children are impotent and ineffective in their walk and in their witness because they have let their guard down and have become defiled by some moral indiscretion.

The apostle Paul fought with all diligence to maintain an unbroken fellowship with God. To the Christians at Corinth he wrote, "But I discipline my body and bring it into subjection, lest, when I have preached to others, I myself should become disqualified" (1 Cor 9:27). The apostle Paul was a missionary statesman, an evangelist, and a preacher; but he was, first of all, a believer-priest. Every child of God is accountable to maintain the sacredness of the spiritual office of the priest.

2. The Significance of the Spiritual Office

A priest is a mediator or one who unites those who have been estranged. The Latin word for priest is *pontifex*, which comes from two words, *pons* meaning "bridge" and *facere* meaning "to make." Thus, *pontifex* means a "bridge maker" or a "bridge builder." A priest is one who builds a bridge between God and man so that communion and fellowship are experienced by both.

In the fullest sense there is only one priest, the Lord Jesus Christ. However, this superior priest ministers in two spheres. In heaven He ministers at the right hand of the Father in His glorified body. On the earth He ministers continually in every place in His mystical body, the church.

When Christ dwelt among men during His incarnation, He spoke God's words and did God's works and walked God's way. However, after His ascension He could no longer be the agent of His priesthood on

earth. Therefore, He created His mystical body, the church, as an extension of His natural body to continue His ministry in the world. Today
every believer is an extension of Christ and His priesthood. Christ has
no other plan for fulfilling His mission in this world except through His
believer-priests.

Years ago, a mother and her young son visited an art gallery where
there was displayed a beautiful painting of Jesus praying in the Garden
of Gethsemane. Visible on the face of Jesus in this particular painting
were tears of passion and concern. The mother asked her son, "Billy, why
do you think Jesus is crying?" With amazing insight, Billy responded,
"Mother, do you see the forms of the three sleeping disciples in the
background? I think Jesus must have been crying because He was concerned that perhaps His disciples would not carry out His mission."

The Lord of glory has entrusted to the believer-priest the responsibility of fulfilling His mission and His ministry on this earth. He has
promised power for every task. The child of God, therefore, is to be an
extension of Jesus Christ into the present century as he endeavors to
continue the work of bridge building, thus making possible communion and fellowship between God and man.

3. The Sphere of the Spiritual Office

The sphere of the administration of the believer-priest has no limitations geographically or chronologically. The child of God is not confined to fulfilling his priestly office only on Sunday or only in the
designated place of worship. Everywhere and at all times the Christian
is to abide in his priesthood. The believer carries his temple with him
and, thus, can worship in his portable, spiritual house day or night,
wherever he is. Constantly from the temple of his own body he can offer
up prayers of intercession. Whatever the location of the body-temple,
the believer-priest has the opportunity of offering worship to God and
rendering service in Jesus' name.

Jesus told His despairing disciples, "Most assuredly, I say to you, he
who believes on me, the works that I do he will do also; and greater

works than these he will do; because I go unto My Father" (Jn 14:12). Jesus was not talking about works that are greater in power, but works that are greater in extent. As millions of believers cover the earth, the extent and the power and the triumph of the message of the cross become greater than in the days of Jesus. There is a sense in which it is better to have the indwelling Holy Spirit in every believer than to have Christ present on earth. Every day the power of deity can be manifested in millions of believers' lives through the indwelling Holy Spirit. The dynamic of the believer-priest's witness was expressed by the apostle Paul who said, "Now unto Him who is able to do exceedingly abundantly above all that we ask or think, according to the power that works in us" (Eph 3:20). With the saints of God daily infiltrating every marketplace, every neighborhood, every campus, every recreational facility, the sphere of this spiritual office is unlimited.

III. A SPIRITUAL SACRIFICE

As was evidenced in the previous chapter, the priest's reason for "entering into the holiest" was that he might make a sacrifice acceptable unto God. Under the Levitical priesthood the offerings which were brought into the tabernacle were animal sacrifices. The offerings of the believer-priests are spiritual sacrifices.

1. The Sacrifice of Penitence

In God's Word there is the mention of many spiritual sacrifices offered to God. First, consider the sacrifice of penitence. It has been said, "To err is understandable; to admit it is unlikely." However, God desires to have His children maintain a humble, broken, contrite spirit. In his great psalm of confession David prayed, "For You do not desire sacrifice, or else would I give it: You do not delight in burnt offering. The sacrifices of God are a broken spirit: a broken and a contrite heart, O God, You will not despise" (Ps 51:16-17).

Always the greatest Christians are the greatest confessors, and the greatest confessors are the greatest Christians. As the believer-priest manifests "a broken and a contrite heart" and becomes transparent before God and men, he places himself in line to receive the blessings of heaven. The child of God may enter boldly into the presence of the Lord, but he may not enter proudly. No one can "enter into the holiest" by his own merits, from which comes pride, but only by the shed blood of Christ. After David's sin he demonstrated a broken spirit and a contrite heart. Believing that God would restore his witness, he said, "Then will I teach transgressors Your ways; and sinners shall be converted to You" (v.13). When the believer-priest offers to God the sacrifice of penitence, God grants to that dear saint a new power, a new vision, a new ministry.

The apostle Paul demonstrated the sacrifice of penitence and brokenness throughout his ministry. He said, "For I am the least of the apostles, who am not worthy to be called an apostle, because I persecuted the church of God" (1 Cor 15:9). Surely his contrite spirit was one of the ingredients the Lord used to make Paul such an anointed, powerful man of God.

The story is told of a seminary graduate who was called to his first church. The acquisition of his theological degree filled him with great self-esteem. On his first Sunday as pastor of the church, this ministerial neophyte strutted into the pulpit with the demeanor of a peacock. He promptly bombed out, laid an ostrich egg, pronounced the benediction, and went slinking down the steps. As he walked to the door to greet the people, he was met first by an old, retired preacher who said, "Son, if you had gone into that pulpit the way you came out you might have come out the way you went in." God desires daily from every New Testament priest the sacrifice of penitence.

2. The Sacrifice of Personality

The sacrifice of personality is the sacrifice of the body, the life, one's entire being. It is a reference to the "living sacrifice" discussed in the previous chapter. This offering is clearly delineated for the believer in

Romans 12:1. The thought of the sacrifice of personality inspires the thought of missionaries who have left not only country and culture, but friends and family to go to a strange and foreign land to serve Christ.

When I was pastor of Eastside Baptist Church in Marietta, Georgia, David Mwangi came to Atlanta to earn a Doctor of Ministry degree at Luther Rice Seminary. He was the Secretary of Education in Kenya and was the pastor of a wonderful church in Nakuru. He was known across his country as a great man of faith and education. He came to our church to apply for a job as a custodian. He won the job, but also won our hearts. His humility and selfless spirit were an inspiration to all of us. He wrote his dissertation on the organization of international mission trips. He inspired and led a mission trip to Kenya and 45 of our church members accompanied Pastor Mwangi on the missionary enterprise. The experience was incredible. Other trips followed. Many Kenyans were saved and blessed by our engagement, but the greatest transformation was among the members of our church who began ministering to the people of Kenya. Our personal involvement among the orphans and impoverished people of Kenya was life changing.

Martin Luther had a dear friend named Friedrich Myconius. For many years they lived in the same monastery. When Luther decided to leave the cloister and answer the Savior's call to fulfill the Great Commission, Myconius promised to pray for Luther's work. He said, "I will remain here amidst the quiet and seclusion of the monastery and pray for you as you minister out in the great world." Myconius was true to his prayer commitment but began to become uncomfortable and restless at night. One night he had a strange dream in which the Savior appeared to him. The Lord showed him His nail-pierced hands and feet and wounded side and said, "Follow me." The vision of the crucified Savior pierced Myconius's heart.

Then the Lord took the young monk to a high mountain and showed him a plain dotted with sheep. One lone shepherd was trying to tend all the sheep. Myconius recognized the shepherd as Martin Luther. The Savior then pointed Myconius to a field of standing corn that stretched all the way to the distant horizon. One lone reaper, Martin Luther, was trying to harvest it all. When Myconius awoke, he said, "It is not enough for me to pray in the solitude of my cloister. The sheep must be shepherded. The field must be harvested. Here am I, Lord, send me."

This dedication is the living sacrifice which the Lord desires. The sacrifice of personality may not require the believer-priest to go to a strange land, but it demands an eternal willingness to go wherever God directs and to do whatever God bids.

3. The Sacrifice of Possessions

The believer-priest should overflow in a wealth of liberality in his giving—so much so that he is willing to make a sacrifice of possessions. The apostle Paul was basking in the sunlight of the generosity of the saints of Philippi when he wrote, "Indeed I have all, and abound: I am full, having received from Epaphroditus the things sent from you, a sweet-smelling aroma, an acceptable sacrifice, well-pleasing to God" (Phil 4:18).

Apparently Epaphroditus was sent to Paul by the Christians of Philippi with a bountiful gift for his ministry. This love offering provided for all of his needs and left him lacking in nothing. The phrase " a sweet-smelling aroma" is a reference primarily not to Paul, but to God's reaction to the generosity expressed by the Philippians. Since the gift was not given primarily to an imprisoned evangelist, but to the glory of God, it was accepted by Paul. In fact, it was as a sweet-smelling savor in the nostrils of God. They had given their property, their possessions sacrificially as an act of worship, as a thank offering to God for the ministry of Paul. God accepted it with a smile of blessing upon His countenance.

In years gone by, believers were often challenged to open three books: their Bibles, their hymnbooks, and their pocketbooks. While younger worshippers read the Scriptures on smart phones and hymn books have been replaced by the lyrics of praise and worship songs projected on media screens the principle remains the same. Remember, however, that the true worshiper should "give. . . not grudgingly, or of necessity: for God loves a cheerful giver" (2 Cor. 9:7). So often the devil will try to convince the believer that it is wrong to take that which is physical and put it in the realm of the spiritual. The devil prefers that the children of God leave their flocks and herds in Egypt (Ex 10:24). Are you prepared to offer your possessions as a "spiritual sacrifice[s], ... acceptable to God"?

4. The Sacrifice of Passion

Under the Old Testament dispensation, the high priest needed to have a compassionate concern for those who ignorantly went astray. The writer of Hebrews avowed, "For every high priest taken from among men is appointed for men in things pertaining to God, that he may offer both gifts and sacrifices for sins. He can have compassion on those who are ignorant and going astray, since he himself is also subject to weakness" (5:1-2). The word "compassion" is a translation of *metriopathed* which means "to have a measure of passion or suffering." The believer-priest is to offer God the sacrifice of a heartfelt compassion and concern for those who are lost in ignorance and deception.

Do you know anything of this passion as a servant of Christ? It was Paul's desire to know Christ "and the power of His resurrection, and the fellowship of His sufferings, being conformed to his death" (Phil 3:10). How many of God's children really want to enter into the passion of Christ, the suffering of Christ? It is doubtful that anyone can ever really know Christ until he begins to feel a burden for the world's need. Three kinds of suffering are mentioned in the Scriptures. There is suffering for sin, which is *chastisement*. There is suffering for Christ, which is *persecution*. However, perhaps the greatest dimension of suffering is suffering with Christ, and that is *passion*. This passion means being identified with the heartthrob of the Son of God for a lost world.

Indeed, Jesus suffered, not in order that we might be saved from suffering, but that we might suffer as He did. Are you prepared to offer to God the sacrifice of passion, the sacrifice of a devoted concern that will cause you to pray like Paul (Rm 9:1-3)?

5. The Sacrifice of Praise

The Holy Spirit exhorts: "Therefore by Him let us continually offer the sacrifice of praise to God, that is, the fruit of our lips, giving thanks to His Name" (Heb 13:15). The Greek word *aineseos*, translated "praise," means "to proclaim one's virtues or excellencies." There is to be a continual hallelujah in the heart and on the lips of the believer-priest. The child of God has much for which to extol the excellencies of the Lord.

The prophet Hosea affirmed "for we will offer the sacrifice of our lips" (Hos 14:2). In the Old Testament the priests would offer cattle to God as a sacrifice. Hosea looked down the corridor of time with the telescope of faith and saw that no calves would be offered for sacrifice, but declared, "We will [offer] the calves of our lips" As the believer approaches God, he extols the excellencies of the Lord Jesus and praises Him for "the mighty gulf that God did span at Calvary."

There is no way to explain why an omnipotent, self-existent God cherishes praise. Why would the eternal God, Creator of the heavens and the earth, condescend to need to be affirmed? Yet, even in the Model Prayer Jesus taught His disciples to pray, "Our Father in heaven, Hallowed be Your name" (Mt 6:9). Jesus indicated that the name of the Lord is to be reverenced, set apart, praised. Indeed, God inhabits the praises of His people (Ps 22:3). He delights to dwell in praise.

In his day, Vance Havner described the mortuary atmosphere of the average church by saying, "Each Sunday in America the clock strikes twelve and the church gives up her dead." Indeed, the pall of death like an ominous cloud hangs over thousands of churches in the land. Sunday by Sunday they perfunctorily go through the forms of worship, but like Samson they "(They) did not know that the Lord had departed from [them]" (Jgs 16:20). Can you imagine a church that majors on form without content?

Here is a suggested caricature of many churches in Havner's day – the 1950s and 60s. Ushers, stoic-like in their demeanor, greet people on Sunday morning with a half grin, half grimace. They mechanically thrust a printed program into the hand of each worshiper. The order of worship is so crowded with litanies and liturgies, collects and collections, hymns and homilies that the likelihood of the Holy Spirit getting into the act is highly suspect.

The choir processes and recesses. The organist's repertoire of Bach, Chopin, and Buxtehude is singularly impressive. There is a time to stand, a time to sit, and a time to kneel. There is a time to sing, a time to recite, a time to respond, and a time to remain silent. The choir sings, "How high on the mountain can the sheep safely graze?" The pastor, Dr. Sounding Brass, waxes eloquently on the latest social issue that has attracted his attention. As the service is concluded, the pastor invites the worshipers to return for a brief vesper service at 5:00 in the chapel.

However, in this 21st century we have sometimes reduced our worship services to casual, colloquial, performance-driven experiences that may be more consumer friendly than God honoring. While we profess to design our worship experiences to please an audience of one – the thrice-holy God of the universe - we may be deceiving ourselves. Alas, many church worship services are planned to please and satisfy the congregation. In fact, some church plants are preceded by a survey of the unchurched in the community to determine what kind of church they would most likely attend. Winston Churchill once said, "Nothing is more dangerous in wartime than to live in the temperamental atmosphere of a Gallup Poll – always taking one's pulse and taking one's temperature." No one should determine the course of his ministry by holding up his finger to find which way the wind is blowing. Why would any church planter allow the unregenerate population of an area dictate the kind of church he should plant?

Many people who attend church today want to hear sermons that require less thinking, that are self-serving and that make fewer demands. There is a consumer mentality in the pew today that prefers sermons that will help the "so called" worshipper: "Learn how to be successful in five easy lessons"; "Discover the four steps to ultimate happiness;" "Employ six simple steps to financial freedom"; and "Find out how to keep the honey in the honeymoon."

No wonder this generation has become known as "The unseeded generation". Do a street survey in your town or community and you will discover that biblical illiteracy is becoming pandemic. That which was true in Samuel's day is also true in our day: "And the word of the Lord was rare in those days; there was no widespread revelation" (1 Sam 3:1, HCSB). In other words, there was no divinely accredited prophet upon whom the anointing of the Lord was known to dwell and who was qualified to proclaim His truth.

We were created to glorify (praise) God. While much of today's praise and worship music is more objective (focusing on God's majesty) than subjective (focusing on man's sinfulness), we must remember to joyfully praise Him not only for His greatness, but for His infallible word. When Paul and Barnabas went to Antioch, they obeyed God's command to preach the Gospel to the Gentiles, and Acts 13:48 declares, "Now when the Gentiles heard this, they were glad and glorified (praised) the word of the Lord." And Dr. Luke reports that many believed and were saved. The Word of God is to be honored, praised, revered, lauded and obeyed. It must be remembered that the sacrifice of praise upon our lips and in our lives is pleasing in the sight of a Holy God.

6. The Sacrifice of Prayer

The constituency of the new priestly order is to offer yet another sacrifice as a sweet savor to God. This final insight into the sacrifices of the New Testament saints is stated in the Book of Revelation.

> "Then another angel, having a golden censer, came and stood at the altar. He was given much incense, that he should offer it with the prayers of all the saints upon the golden altar which was before the throne. And the smoke of the incense, with the prayers of the saints, ascended before God from the angel's hand" (8:3-4).

The Apostle John pictures the prayers of the redeemed which are ascending to God. The "smoke of the incense" indicates the finished work of Christ. Thankfully, the prayers of the believers ascend to heaven with the incense, all made possible by the finished work of the Savior.

In Ephesians, the apostle Paul wrote, "And walk in love, as Christ also has loved us and given himself for us, an offering and a sacrifice to God for a sweet-smelling aroma" (5:2). What Jesus did on the cross was so satisfying to God, it was like sweet-smelling incense. The prayers of the saints often seem so ineffective and so poorly articulated, but every child of God should remember that God adds to those prayers the incense of the finished work of the Lord Jesus. Every sincere prayer, therefore, enters into the presence of God, not on its own merit but on the basis of what Jesus did at Calvary.

These are the spiritual sacrifices to be continually offered to a Holy God by the believer-priest from his portable temple. Once again it is evident that for every priestly privilege there is a royal responsibility.

Note

1. Charles Haddon Spurgeon, *The Treasury of the Bible, Vol. 4, The New Testament*, (Grand Rapids: Zondervan Publications, 1968), p. 380.

7

The Believer-Priest and the Word of God (Malachi 2:4-9)

As a college student at Mercer University, I had the blessed privilege of being the preacher on youth revival teams. On one occasion our team had the opportunity to minister in the Druid Hills Baptist Church in Atlanta, Georgia, during the pastorate of Dr. Louie D. Newton. One night after the worship service, our revival team heard the story of an unusual experience that had occurred in the life of the Druid Hills Church.

One year during the Christmas holidays the college students were scheduled to lead a Sunday evening worship service. Those responsible for planning the program wanted to have a college freshman give a testimony. The purpose of this particular testimony was to affirm the fact that God's grace is sufficient for the beginning of a new life away from home on the university campus.

The first student asked to fill this slot on the program was a strong and committed Christian but was extremely shy. This young man declined the invitation to be on the program, citing his timidity as the reason for refusing. He had used the first months of college to refine his faith and strengthen his convictions, but the thought of speaking to hundreds of people paralyzed him with fear.

The second student asked to accept this responsibility was an extreme extrovert. He had gone away to college and had become enamored with the "liberal" arts education of the school he attended. Fascinated with the "higher criticism" of Wellhausen, he had begun to depart from the faith he had been taught as a child. However, his desire to be heard prompted him to accept the invitation to speak at the student-led worship service.

When the night came for the students to lead in worship, this brash young extrovert stood to speak. With a cynical sneer he launched an attack on the institutional church, belittled the faith of the fathers, and castigated what he called the "narrow-mindedness" of Christianity. Then, with brazen audacity, he dared anyone to refute his allegations.

The congregation sat in stunned silence for what seemed an eternity. At last, the shy, but committed student who had declined to speak, stood in the back of the worship center. With a trembling voice he began to speak the only words that came to his mind – the words of an old hymn:

> Stand up, stand up for Jesus,
> Ye soldiers of the cross;
> Lift high his royal banner,
> it must not suffer loss:
> From vict'ry unto vict'ry
> his army shall he lead,
> Till every foe is vanquished,
> And Christ is Lord indeed.

We were told that before the bashful freshman had recited the first verse of that old hymn, people started to stand throughout the congregation and that by the time the recitation was completed, the entire church was standing to affirm their faith in the Word of God and the Lord of life.

What is to be the attitude of the believer-priest toward the Word of God today? Does finite man have the prerogative to decide which portion of Scripture is infallible and which portion is not infallible? Does soul liberty give to the New Testament priest the license to accept certain passages of Scripture and reject others? Is the Bible inspired only in spots and are believers inspired to spot the spots?

In the Old Testament God expected the priests to have a high regard for His Word. When the priests did anything to dilute or discredit the law of God by lip or life, they incurred the displeasure of Jehovah. The Lord's message to the priests of the Old Testament through Malachi is applicable to believer-priests today.

I. A COMMITTED PRIESTHOOD

God was speaking of a committed priesthood when He declared:

> Then you shall know that I have sent this commandment to you, that my covenant with Levi may continue, says the Lord of hosts. My covenant was with him, one of life and peace, and I gave them to him that he might fear Me; so, he feared Me and was reverent before My name. The law of truth was in his mouth, and injustice was not found on his lips. He walked with Me in peace and equity, and turned many away from iniquity (Mal 2:4-6).

In these verses Malachi contrasted the deplorable conduct of the ungodly priests of his day with the commendable character and committed lifestyle of the sons of Levi in the early days of the Old Testament priesthood.

Levi, the son of Jacob, had no particular quality that made him an obvious choice for the priesthood. Levi and his brother Simeon had taken vengeance into their own hands and killed a man for raping their sister. Therefore, Jacob cursed these two sons for their anger and cruelty. He predicted that their descendants would be scattered throughout the tribes of Israel (Gn 49:7).

It seems strange that God would choose the descendants of Levi to serve as priests. However, a study of the tribe of Levi produces evidence of their faithfulness to God and their fidelity to His Word.

For example, when the children of Israel fell into an idolatrous orgy and worshiped the golden calf, Moses realized the situation called for drastic action. He interrupted that abominable pagan ritual by calling for "a division of the house." He said, "Whoever is on the Lord's side - come unto me!" (Ex 32:26). Consequently, ". . . all the sons of Levi gathered themselves together to him" (v. 26). Apparently, the sons of Levi had not indulged in the mad merriment, the naked sensualism, and the foolish idolatry that threatened to consume the nation. Thus, having taken their stand on the Lord's side, the sons of Levi were put to a most severe test by Moses. "And he said to them, Thus says the Lord God of Israel: let every man put his sword on his side, and go in and out from entrance to entrance throughout the camp, and let every man kill his brother, and every man his companion, and every man his neighbor" (v. 27).

This stern command would have provoked rebellion within the hearts of many people. However, in the response of the tribe of Levi there was no reluctance, no hesitation, and no argument. There was a willingness and a readiness to do the will of God. The Word of God reports: "So the sons of Levi did according to the word of Moses" (v. 28).

Later when Moses was about to die, he gathered the tribes of Israel around him and committed a legacy to each one. To the tribe of Levi Moses gave this blessing:

> Let Your Thummim and Your Urim be with Your holy one,
> Whom you tested at Massah, and with whom You contended at the waters of Meribah, Who says of his father
> and mother, 'I have not seen them'; Nor did he acknowledge his brothers, or know his own children; for they have

observed Your word and kept Your covenant. They shall teach Jacob your judgments, and Israel Your law. They shall put incense before You, and a whole burnt sacrifice on Your altar (Dt 33:8-10).

1. The Communication of a Committed Priesthood

Malachi made reference to the early days of the Levitical priestly order when he extolled the virtues of a committed priesthood. He wrote, "The law of truth was in his mouth" (Mal 2:6). This commendation was probably directed toward Phinehas, the grandson of Aaron (Ex 6:25; Nm 25:7). This zealous servant of God turned the wrath of God away from the children of Israel by securing the cessation of a plague that threatened to destroy the nation. For the action of Phinehas in behalf of the children of Israel, God rewarded him with a "covenant of peace" (Nm 25:12). This covenant was God's assurance that the priesthood would remain in the family of Phinehas forever (v. 13). If the words, "the law of truth was in his mouth," referred to Phinehas, they make him a pattern for the person who would be a truly committed priest.

The true priest has an uncompromising allegiance to the Word of God. He has saturated his mind and spirit with the truth of God. The law of the Lord is his delight (Ps 119:174). The Holy Scriptures have become a veritable lamp unto his feet and a light unto his pathway (v. 105).

The committed priest realizes that his responsibility is to represent God to man. Since God and His Word are inseparably linked together, the true priest will become intimately acquainted with the Word of God. He will closely identify with the Scriptures so that he might clearly and accurately represent God to man. To know and believe the Word of God is to know God Himself. Indeed, "faith comes by hearing, and hearing by the word of God" (Rm 10:17).

There remains such a union between God and His Word that whatever the Scripture says, God said. In fact, the apostle Paul felt free to personify the Scripture as if it were God speaking. Galatians 3:8 is an example of the apostle actually personifying the Scripture. Speaking of Scripture being the voice of God, Paul exclaimed, "And the scripture, foreseeing that God would justify the Gentiles by faith, preached the gospel unto Abraham beforehand, saying, 'In you all nations shall be blessed.'"

In the Book of Exodus God said to Pharaoh, "For this purpose have I raised you up" (9:16). However, in Romans 9:17, Paul wrote, "For the scripture says to Pharaoh, "For this same very purpose have I raised you up." In one place, "God says," and in another place "the Scripture says." Thus, when the Scripture speaks, God speaks. God is the author of what Scripture records. The totality of Scripture was summed up by Paul in the phrase, "The oracles of God" (Rm 3:2). The Bible is the Word of God and is inseparably linked with God.

To know the Word of God and to live in the Word of God is to know God Himself. The results of having the Spirit of God dwell within (Eph 5:18-21) and the result of having the Word of God dwell within (Col 3:16-17) are amazingly similar. The committed priest will baptize his heart and mind in the Holy Scriptures.

In that trysting place the saint of God will find that the Word of God is ever feeding, shaping, molding, and directing the thoughts, the actions, and the reactions of his life.

Then, fresh from the presence of God and illuminated by the Holy Spirit, the priest can reveal the heart and mind of God to all those in need of His ministry. He can bear witness of the Lord's transcendent beauty. With authority he can proclaim the excellencies of God's virtues. The believer-priest who has met the Lord in the sacred Word can turn from that experience to lift up his voice like a trumpet (Is 58:1). A trumpet has the crisp, clear sound of authenticity and reality.

Alas, there are too many who give out the sound of a piccolo. However, if the Word of God does not abide in the heart, it will never make an impression on the life or find expression from the lips. With a persuasiveness born of a personal experience, the true priest can communicate the "law of truth."

Malachi was probably referring to Phinehas once again when he avowed that "iniquity was not found on his lips." With "the law of truth ... in his mouth," it was inconceivable that he would have "injustice... in his lips" (2:6). Why? The Word of God is a bulwark against sin. The psalmist declared, "Your word I have hidden in my heart, that I might not sin against You" (Ps 119:11).

In the year King Uzziah died, Isaiah saw "the Lord sitting on a throne, high and lifted up" (Is 6:1). In the light of the thrice Holy God of Israel, Isaiah saw his own wretchedness and wickedness. The thoughts of his own sinfulness seemed to focus upon his mouth. He said, "I am a man of unclean lips, and I dwell in the midst of a people of unclean lips" (v. 5). With the lips and the mouth there is a great potential for good or evil.

The Bible declares, "Lying lips are an abomination to the Lord" (Prv 12:22). The writer of Ecclesiastes avowed, "but the lips of a fool shall swallow him up" (10:12). The wise penman of the Proverbs stated, "A fool's mouth is his destruction, and his lips are the snare of his soul" (18:7).

The lips of man can also be used to bless and encourage. The writer of Proverbs affirmed that "the lips of the righteous feed many" (10:21). "The truthful lip shall be established forever: but a lying tongue is but for a moment" (12:19). "Righteous lips are the delight of kings; and they love him who speaks what is right" (16:13).

The true priest guards his lips against words that are cruel and inconsiderate. Profanity must never proceed from his mouth. Of Jesus it was said, "Gracious words... proceeded out of His mouth" (Lk 4:22). The believer-priest should guard his words and seek to order his conversation after the Lord.

Since the priest represents God to man, he should be free of all shams and theories, hold to stern doctrinal integrity, and forever seek to "rightly dividing the word of truth" (2 Tm 2:15). His communication of divine revelation must never be the product of "cunningly devised fables" (2 Pt 1:16), or a "private interpretation" (v. 20). The believer-priest must remember that "holy men of God spoke as they were moved by the

Holy Spirit" (v. 21). The communication of a committed priest fosters neither doubt nor defilement. Conversely, it inspires faith and fidelity.

2. The Conduct of a Committed Priesthood

God spoke of the exemplary priest of the Old Testament when He said, "He walked with me in peace and equity" (Mal 2:6). The life of the committed priest should be marked by a consistent walk with God. In his Ephesians letter, Paul emphasized the importance of the walk of the Christian. First, the apostle described the position of the believer with Christ in the heavenlies. He reminded the saint of who he is in Christ. In Christ, the believer is rich and has "obtained an inheritance" (1:11). The child of God is a king, a priest, and a joint heir with Jesus Christ.

Furthermore, Paul moved from the *wealth* of the believer to the *walk* of the believer. He admonished, "I, therefore, the prisoner of the Lord, beseech you to walk worthy of the calling with which you were called with all lowliness and gentleness" (4:1-2). The word "walk" is used eight times in Ephesians. The characteristics of a worthy walk are given in chapter 4:1-6, 9. Basically the believer-priest is to maintain a step-by-step process of constant growth into Christlikeness. Or, as Paul similarly writes to the Colossians, "As you therefore have received Christ Jesus the Lord, so walk in him" (Col 2:6).

Notice that the walk was "in peace and equity" (Mal 2:6). These words seem to characterize an intimate, harmonious walk. Amos, the prophet, suggested that when two walk together they are in agreement and share a common goal or destination (Am 3:3).

In 2 Kings 23:3, Josiah made a covenant "to follow the Lord." However, to walk with the Lord suggests an even greater affection and companionship. Phinehas and other priests of the Old Testament dispensation were committed to walk with God.

3. The Consequences of a Committed Priesthood

When the communication and the conduct of the Levitical priestly order were right, the consequences were exhilarating. Malachi reported that such a committed priesthood "turned many away from iniquity" (2:6). The true priest not only lives to walk in sweet communion with God but also desires to lead others in the path of righteousness.

Indeed, the believer is to witness. He is to proclaim the gospel verbally; however, his first matter of concern is to live in holiness and godliness. A Christlike life will "turn many away from iniquity."

When Paul wrote Timothy, he exhorted, "Take heed to yourself, and (then) to the doctrine" (1 Tm 4:16). Timothy was instructed to give first consideration to his own heart and life. Paul then referred to the matter of doctrinal integrity. The Greek word translated "doctrine" is *didaskaliai* and denotes the teaching of Timothy. Paul instructed his son in the ministry to maintain the order of "yourself first and (then) to the doctrine." Then Paul charged him "continue in them: for in doing this you will save both yourself and those who hear you."

Jesus said to His disciples, "and you shall be witnesses to Me" (Ac 1:8). The believer, living under the new priestly order, must be a witness before he does any witnessing. "Being" always precedes "doing." Christians must always beware of the abomination of high doctrine and low conduct, remembering that a godly life will "turn many away from iniquity."

Peter is a good example of a life transformed by the power of God. After Peter was filled with the Spirit, he did not always have to speak in order to affect someone's life. In fact, Acts 5 relates: "And believers were increasingly added to the Lord, multitudes of both men and women, so that they brought the sick out into the streets, and laid them on beds and couches, that at the least the shadow of Peter passing by might fall on some of them" (vv. 14-15). Peter was a part of the new priestly order, and his life demonstrated the consequences of a committed priesthood.

4. The Continuation of a Committed Priesthood

Through Malachi, God declared, "For the lips of a priest should keep knowledge, and people should seek the law from his mouth: for he is the messenger of the Lord of hosts" (2:7). Phinehas, typifying the integrity of the first Levitical priests, became a pattern for all succeeding priests. Through Malachi, God stated His expectations of the priesthood. He ardently desired to have the commitment and faithfulness of the early priesthood continue. God declared, "The lips of the priest should keep knowledge." The priests were guardians of the sacred deposits of truth. The priests, of all men, were to defend the faith and contend for the purity of the Word of God.

Today countless churches are infiltrated by apostasy. They have jettisoned the virgin birth, the physical resurrection of Christ, the personal, visible return of Christ, and the inspiration, infallibility and sufficiency of the Scriptures. Knowing by divine inspiration that such a time would come, Jude, the half-brother of Jesus, wrote an epistle to tell believers how they should live in the last days of apostasy.

Jude exhorted, "Beloved, while I was very diligent to write to you concerning your common salvation, I found it necessary to write to you exhorting you to contend earnestly for the faith which was once for all delivered to the saints" (v. 3). Notice the phrase "contend earnestly." As believers we are in a war against Satan personally, but we are also in a struggle to defend the purity of the faith. The root word for "contend" is *agon* from which we get our word agony. This Greek word has to do with a struggle; but when it first came into existence, it meant "a stadium" or "a bowl"—the place of a contest. Earnestly contending for the faith is like playing in a spiritual super bowl throughout our entire Christian lives.

The true priest will forever fight for "the faith which was once delivered to the saints." Paul used the same word in 1 Timothy 6:12, when he said, "Fight the good fight of faith." If the priest is to represent God to man, he must zealously protect the Word of God and defend its purity at all costs.

Furthermore, God said that the people should rightly expect to hear God's law from the mouth of the priest. The priests, of all people, should be the disseminators of divine truth. God said, "People should seek the law from his mouth" (Mal 2:7). God told Aaron, "You may teach the children of Israel all the statutes which the Lord has spoken unto them" (Lv 10:11). The priest should so study the law and faithfully teach it that the people will be encouraged to come to him for help.

The story is told of a rancher who owned hundreds of sheep. Each evening he called the sheep at feeding time by striking a triangle with a metal bar. The rancher's ten-year-old son often watched in amazement as the sheep hurriedly made their way across the hillside to the barn where the food was waiting for them.

One day when his father was gone to town on an errand, the curious son decided to see if the sheep would come at his signal. He struck the triangle with the steel bar as his dad had struck it hundreds of times. To the lad's delight, the sheep came as they always had when the signal echoed across the hills.

As the boy stood surrounded by bleating sheep, the father drove up in his truck and promptly gave the child the thrashing of his life. When his crying subsided, the tearful lad asked, "Dad, why did you spank me? I called the sheep just like you do."

The father sternly replied, "Son, I didn't spank you for calling the sheep, but for calling them and not feeding them."

The regenerate and the unregenerate should expect to hear the Word of God from the mouth of the priest, and they should hear it in all of its purity and in all of its quickening power. Why should the people expect the priest to be a depository of truth and a declarer of divine truth? Malachi said, "He is the messenger of the Lord of hosts" (2:7). Today every believer is a member of the new priestly order. Therefore, every saint of God is to be a messenger of the Lord. Paul declared, "We are ambassadors for Christ" (2 Cor 5:20).

The cry of the psalmist was, "Let the redeemed of the Lord say so" (Ps 107:2). As Aaron was a messenger of the Lord, the twentieth-century Christian is to be a messenger of the Lord. Herein is the call for the continuation of a committed priesthood.

II. A COMPROMISING PRIESTHOOD

The priests of Malachi's day drifted far from the ideal which God had established when He instituted the Levitical priesthood. They strayed from the path of righteousness. Their teaching caused many to stumble. They corrupted the covenant which God had made with Levi. Their priesthood did not follow in the tradition of the good and godly Phinehas.

1. The Communication of a Compromising Priesthood

One charge against the priests in the text is that they had "caused many to stumble at the law." Both by their teaching and their example, they had caused many to err. These priests had also "corrupted the covenant of Levi" (Mal 2:8).

The Pulpit Commentary suggests that this refers to a "tampering with the Word of God, to employ it to support some favorite prejudice, or to buttress their little sect."[1] S. Franklin Logsdon said, "They simply became self-opinionated concerning its precepts superimposing their own interpretations and granting themselves leniency and latitude in applying it to their lives."[2]

When the infallible Word of God is diluted, it becomes of no effect. This was the concern of Charles H. Spurgeon during the *Down Grade Controversy* in the Baptist Union of England in the latter part of the 19th century. Spurgeon was concerned about theological errors which had crept into the Baptist Union. He traced the errors to "a want of adequate faith in the divine inspiration of the sacred Scriptures."[3] Though the British Baptist Union voted to censure Spurgeon at their assembly in April 1888, the famed pastor continued to stand upon the integrity of the Word of God.

In Spurgeon's autobiography he wrote:

> Before my conversion, I was accustomed to reading the
> Scriptures to admire their grandeur, to feel the charm of

their history, and wonder at the majesty of their language; but I altogether missed the Lord's intent therein. But when the Spirit came with His divine life, and quickened all the Book to my newly-enlightened soul, the inner meaning shone forth with wondrous glory. I was not in a frame of mind to judge God's Word, but I accepted it without demur; I did not venture to sit in judgment upon my Judge and become the advisor of the unerring God. Whatever I found to be in His Word, I received with intense joy.[4]

Much of the controversy swirling about the great evangelical denominations today has centered on the infallibility of the Scriptures. Dr. W. A. Criswell, the late and legendary pastor of the First Baptist Church of Dallas, Texas, speaking at the Southern Baptist Convention Pastors' Conference in Dallas in 1985, referred to the *Down Grade Controversy* of the British Baptist Union. Then Dr. Criswell said, "As with the Baptists of Great Britain, whether we continue to live or ultimately die lies in our dedication to the infallible Word of God."

Some contend that historically Baptists have held to the concept of soul competency or soul liberty, allowing that God has given to every person the right to interpret the Scriptures for himself. One must remember, however, that liberty is not license, and soul liberty historically was never understood to mean that one could freely believe contrary to his church's doctrinal statement and still be its salaried servant.

In addressing this issue in his book, *Why I Am a Baptist*, Louie D. Newton wrote:

We do not think that men are at liberty to think of the Bible or not, to obey it or not, just as they please. But we think that they are bound to use their judgment, and to govern it, by the facts and truths of the Bible. The liberty that we claim, is not to follow our own fancies, or predilections, in investigating the Bible, not merely to speculate upon it, and then diverge from its teachings if we choose to do so, because that would be criminal trifling. The right to investigate the truth does not carry with it the right to disobey it, or to doubt it, — that would convert the doctrine into rebellion against its author, which is an evil, and cannot become a right.[5]

The believer-priest, illuminated by the Holy Spirit, has the right to interpret the Scripture for himself. He does not have the right to add anything or subtract anything from the Word of God (Rv 22:18-19). Furthermore, he has the responsibility of communicating the truth of God in a clear, forthright manner. The Bible says, "If the trumpet gives an uncertain sound, who shall prepare himself to the battle?" (2 Cor 14:8).

In the last quarter of the 20th century the Southern Baptist Convention was torn by a controversy over the infallibility of Holy Scripture. Many Baptist colleges and seminaries were plagued with liberalism. When I went to Mercer University, I was told that since I was a ministerial student, I needed to take German as my foreign language, because the great theologians that were being studied at that school were the Neo-Orthodox German theologians who taught a higher critical approach to understanding the Bible. At that point I began to see first-hand the curse, the rot, the virus and the corruption of liberalism.

When Adrian Rogers, pastor of Bellevue Baptist Church in Memphis, was elected the Southern Baptist Convention president in 1979 the Conservative Resurgence was officially launched. The conservatives and the moderates (liberals) worked hard to get their candidates elected as president of the convention, because those who were elected to that office had the constitutional authority to appoint the committee that ultimately had the responsibility to see that their representatives were nominated to serve as trustees of SBC seminaries and the other entities.

In those days the schism in the convention was obvious. One could cut the tension at the annual meetings with a knife. A Peace Committee was formed to see if the two factions could co-exist and find common ground. In one of the meetings of that committee, Adrian Rogers stated,

I am willing to compromise about many things, but not the Word of God. So far as getting together is concerned, we don't have to get together. The Southern Baptist Convention, as it is, does not have to survive. I don't have to be the pastor of Bellevue Baptist Church. I don't have to be loved. I don't have to live. But I will not compromise the Word of God." (Adrian Rogers never gave an uncertain sound. Every Baptist, particularly the pastors, missionaries, evangelists and denominational servants should never let his name die. Get his books. Listen to his sermons. Remember him as one of our most honored men of God).

The truth of the matter is that when the pulpit and the pew fail to sound forth the trumpet of truth, they expose themselves to the judgment of God. Consider God's words to Ezekiel: "Son of man, I have made you a watchman for the house of Israel; therefore hear a word from My mouth, and give them warning from Me: [18] When I say to the wicked, 'You shall surely die,' and you give him no warning, nor speak to warn the wicked from his wicked way, to save his life, that same wicked *man* shall die in his iniquity; but his blood I will require at your hand" (Ez 3:17-18).

These verses reveal the tragedy of prophets and priests who fail to communicate the word of life to those lost in sin.

2. The Conduct of a Compromising Priest

The priests of Malachi's day were "departed from the way" (Mal 2:8). They had deserted God's chosen path for them and had substituted their own humanly devised way. Instead of helping men accept the truth and live God honoring lives, the priesthood had become an impediment to men finding the Lord. Rather than being an avenue to God, as Jesus came to be, they were a roadblock, an obstacle.

The apostle Paul addressed this very issue in his letter to the church in Rome. He declared, "Therefore let us not judge one another anymore: but rather resolve this, not to put a stumbling block or a cause to fall in

our brother's way" (Rm 14:13). If the believer has an intimate relationship to God, he will live in such a way that his relationship to others is
enhanced. If there is a flaw in the character of the believer, he becomes
a stumbling block rather than a stepping-stone.

All life is either centripetal or centrifugal Centripetal means to
gather or move toward a central point. Centrifugal means to scatter or
move away from an axis or central point. Jesus said, "He who is not with
Me is against me, and he who does not gather with Me scatters abroad"
(Mt 12:30). The world carefully observes the walk of a child of God. If
that walk is consistently Christlike, those who observe it will be drawn
to Christ. However, if the believer's performance doesn't measure up to
his profession, his hypocrisy will be apparent, and he will turn many
away from the cause of Christ.

As a Christian, is your life centripetal or centrifugal? Are you gathering for Christ or scattering from Christ?

The lost man in the office is carefully watching the Christian to see
if he will participate in the telling of off-color jokes, to see if he will
join the others in betting on the ball game, to see if he will take that
social drink at the office party. The lost woman in the community is ob-
serving that Christian mother next door to see if she gossips about the
neighbors, to see if she loses her temper with her children, to see if she
lives a consistent Christian life.

The televangelist has his sphere of influence. The pastor of the local
church has his sphere of influence. Likewise, the Christian businessper-
son, the saved homemaker, the redeemed farmer, the converted candlestick maker, all have their spheres of influence. Each individual lives
and works within his own concentric circle. Within that circle, however
large or small it may be, the believer-priest is to be the salt that saves
and that arrests corruption and the light that dispels darkness. How
tragic when the Christian is a stumbling block rather than a stepping-
stone!

3. The Consequences of a Compromising Priest

Priests who "are departed from the way" (Mal 2:8) adversely affect the lives of others and bring the judgment of God upon themselves. Jeremiah decried this deplorable condition when he wrote, "A horrible and shocking thing has happened in the land: The prophets prophesy lies, the priests rule by their own authority, and my people love it this way. But what will you do in the end?" (Jer 5:30-31, NIV).

The people of the world are forever looking for the preacher to water down the gospel. They are continually hoping to find a chink in the armor of some Christian. They love to see a Christian fall because it dilutes their sense of guilt over sin. The believer-priest must live like Noah, who condemned the world of his day by his faithfulness and righteousness.

Alas, Christians often fail miserably to lift up the standard of righteousness. Therefore, they cause many to stumble. Jesus said, "If the blind leads the blind, both will fall into the ditch" (Mt 15:14). It is bad enough for one person to stumble and fall, but for that one to be the occasion for others to stumble and fall is doubly tragic, eternally tragic. The extent of the tragedy is expressed by Christ who said, "But whosoever causes one of these little ones who believes in Me to sin, it would be better for him if a millstone were hung around his neck, and he were drowned in the depth of the sea" (Mt 18:6).

To conclude the matter, God called such stumbling-block priests "contemptible and base" (Mal 2:9). That which was honorable and noble in the ideal had become disgraceful and ignoble in actuality; for example, God had chosen Eli and his house to walk before Him in the service of the priesthood. Eli's sons disgraced his name and his house. Thus, God declared, "Those who honor Me I will honor; and those who despise Me shall be lightly esteemed" (1 Sm 2:30, NIV).

The believer-priest must forever saturate his soul in the Word of God. He must live it consistently and communicate it powerfully. After all, it is the solemn responsibility of the priest to represent God to man and he must do so by precept and by example.

Notes

1. H. D. Spence and Joseph S. Exell, *The Pulpit Commentary Vol. 14, Am-Malachi* (Grand Rapids: William B. Eerdman Publishing, 1950), p. 35.

2. S. Franklin Logsdon, *Malachi: Will a Man Rob God* (Chicago: Moody Press, 1961), p. 47.

3. L. Russ Bush and Tom Nettles, *Baptists and the Bible* (Chicago: Moody Bible Institute, 1980), p. 247.

4. Ibid., p. 253.

5. Louie D. Newton, *Why I Am a Baptist* (New York: Thomas Nelson & Sons, 1957), p. 39.

8

The Believer-Priest and Prayer (1 Timothy 2:1,3)

In the previous chapter consideration was given to the fact that the believer-priest has the responsibility of representing God to men. As the New Testament saint studies the Word of God, dwells in the Word of God, and saturates his soul with the Word of God, he is able to communicate the Word of God to others by precept and by example. The child of God studies the Scripture, not in order to become a depository of truth, but to become a dispenser of truth. Paul instructed Timothy, "The things that you have heard of me among many witnesses, commit these to faithful men, who will be able to teach others also" (2 Tm 2:2). In this way the believer is able to represent God, who is inseparably linked to His Word.

Conversely, as an intercessor, the believer-priest is able to represent men to God. Since the way of access into the presence of the Father has been opened up by the shed blood of the Son of God, the child of God has the privilege of praying directly to the Heavenly Father. "For through Him [Jesus Christ] we both have access by one Spirit unto the Father" (Eph 2:18). The Scripture teaches that prayer is to be offered to the Father in the Spirit and through the Son. What a glorious privilege and what a solemn responsibility it is to stand before God on behalf of others!

I. THE PRIVILEGE OF PRAYER

In the Sermon on the Mount, Jesus proclaimed, "Ask, and it will be given to you; seek, and you will find; knock, and it will be opened to you, For everyone who asks receives; and he who seeks finds, and to him who knocks it will be opened" (Mt 7:7-8). These words constitute a glorious prayer promise from the Son of God. Is it a universal promise? Can anyone pray and expect God to answer? Has God inclined His ear to all people everywhere?

Indeed, not everyone who prays can anticipate a heavenly response. The Bible teaches that the promises of God are to His children. The Sermon on the Mount was addressed to the disciples of Jesus (Mt 5:1-2). Those who believe on Christ are the ones offered the privilege of asking, seeking, and knocking at the throne of God.

1. The Prayer of a Sinner

Is communion with God totally beyond the reach of an unbeliever? Can a sinner present his petitions to the Lord and expect an answer? The Bible seems to indicate that the unbeliever cannot approach God. Paul strongly intimated this when he asked, "For what fellowship has righteousness with lawlessness? and what communion has light with darkness" (2 Cor 6:14). The writer of Hebrews declared, "But without faith it is impossible to please Him, for he who comes to God must believe that He is, and that He is a rewarder of those who diligently seek him" (Heb 11:6).

Faith in the Son of God is the basis upon which one may approach the throne of God. Jesus said, "I am the way, the truth, and the life. No one comes to the Father except through Me" (Jn 14:6). God's prayer promises are exclusively to His children. Indeed, believers are taught to pray, "Our Father in heaven" (Mt 6:9). Furthermore, God says to us in I Timothy 2:5: "For there is one God and one mediator between God and men, the man Christ Jesus."

Suppose, for example, there was a time years ago when my twin sons came to me as teenagers and requested that I buy them new tennis shoes. Upon investigating the matter, I discovered that their only tennis shoes are worn, torn, and tattered almost beyond recognition. With an awareness of their acute need for tennis shoes, I took the boys to the local department store and purchased two pairs of double-stitched, triple-cushioned, air-spring, victory-guaranteed tennis shoes. The twins proudly wore their spanking-new shoes home from the store. Then within a matter of minutes all the neighborhood boys gathered in our yard to admire the twin's tennis shoes.

Suppose one boy looked at me and said, "Mr. Harris, would you buy me some shoes just like the ones you bought John and Jerry?" The truth is that if the neighborhood boy really needed tennis shoes, and his parents couldn't afford to buy him shoes, and if I had the money to purchase them for him and was in a particularly generous mood, I just might buy him some new shoes. However, I would not likely feel the same obligation to supply the needs of all the neighbors' children that I felt to supply the needs of my own children.

God is gracious and He may, in love, occasionally respond to the request of an unbeliever and supply some temporal blessing. However, God is not obligated by any promise to answer the prayer of an unbeliever, except the prayer for salvation. The unregenerate soul cannot approach the throne of grace in Jesus' name or on the basis of the promises of God and expect to receive an answer.

However, when some poor, unredeemed sinner gets under the Holy Spirit's convicting power, humbles himself before God, and prays for deliverance from sin, God inclines His ear to hear that prayer. The publican bowed contritely before God and prayed, "God, be merciful to me a sinner" (Lk 18:13). God answered the publican's prayer because the Scripture states that he went home "justified."

The prayer of the sinner seeking salvation will always be heard. God is "not willing that any should perish but that all should come to repentance" (2 Pt 3:9). In fact, He promises, "For whoever calls on the name of the Lord shall be saved" (Rm 10:13). The prayer of the sinner is scarcely a prayer at all. It is more like the cry of a drowning man. A loving God could not very well turn a deaf ear to one in such eternal peril. Every saint who ever cried to God for deliverance from sin should zealously encourage every sinner to voice the same plaintive plea to God. This prayer is the only petition of the unbeliever God has promised to answer.

2. The Prayer of the Saint

The believer has the privilege of praying with authority. However, the child of God needs to clearly understand who he is in Christ Jesus. Paul prayed that the Christians of Ephesus might understand their throne rights as believers. His supplication was that: "the God of our Lord Jesus Christ, the Father of glory, may give to you the spirit of wisdom and revelation in the knowledge of Him, the eyes of your understanding being enlightened; that you may know what is the hope of His calling, what are the riches of the glory of His inheritance in the saints, and what is the exceeding greatness of His power toward us who believe, according to the working of His mighty power" (Eph 1:17-19).

The believer is a royal blue blood. He is a child of the King. He is a partaker of the divine nature. He is indwelt by the Holy Spirit. He is led by the Spirit. His citizenship is in heaven. He is an heir of God and a joint heir with Jesus Christ. He has been made to sit in heavenly places in Christ.

Furthermore, God delights to bless His children. David joyfully declared: "In Your presence is fulness of joy; at Your right hand are pleasures for evermore" (Ps 16:11). He has promised that He will withhold nothing good from those who walk uprightly (Ps 84:11).

Too frequently the believer lives far beneath his privileges as a member of the royal family of God. He is too satisfied with too little. Many believers are content to live like spiritual paupers when they could live like spiritual princes. In prayer the believer has the privilege of linking himself with omnipotence and drawing from the resources of the Creator of the universe.

The saint of God doesn't have to sheepishly approach God as a beggar would. He may confidently enter into the presence of God as a child of the King. The privilege of prayer is that the believer-priest has access to God. Prayer is "having the boldness to enter into the Holiest by the blood of Jesus" (Heb 10:19). Prayer is entering into "the secret place of the Most High" and "abid(ing) under the shadow of the Almighty" (Ps 91:1). Prayer is understanding one's position and one's possessions in Christ Jesus. Prayer is learning to relate to God, not as some vague impersonal distant deity, but as a loving, compassionate, ever-present Father.

II. THE PLATEAUS OF PRAYER

Indeed, the believer is a priest with certain throne rights. As a New Testament priest, the child of God has access to the Father and may exercise this privilege through prayer. There appears to be a progression in prayer, even as there is a progression in the life of the maturing Christian. As the believer grows in his faith, he grows in his prayer life. In the growth process he ascends the mountain of prayer and is constantly moving to higher ground through the plateaus of petition, intercession, and communion.

1. The Prayer of Petition

Someone has said that the prayer of petition is the "gimme" stage of prayer. That evaluation of the first plateau of prayer may be somewhat accurate, but the petitionary prayer is not to be depreciated. Petition means "to ask, to solicit, to make a request." In the prayer of petition, one makes a request of God. It is perfectly right to do so because God throughout His Word urges the believer to pray the prayer of petition. He declared, "Yet you do not have because you do not ask" (Jas 4:2).

"Now this is the confidence that we have in Him, that if we ask anything according to His will, He hears us. And if we know that He hears
us, whatever we ask, we know that we have the petitions that we have
asked of Him" (1 Jn 5:14-15). "If any of you lacks wisdom let him ask of
God" (Jas 1:5). "Be anxious for nothing, but in everything by prayer and
supplication, with thanksgiving, let your requests be made known to
God" (Phil 4:6).

One of the reasons God desires His children to make their requests
known to Him is because doing so indicates the child's dependence
upon the Father.

I recall with unmeasured joy numerous incidents out of the childhood of our twins. One such incident occurred on a Saturday evening
when the boys were about four years old. I was making certain physical
preparations for the Lord's day. I had just shined my shoes and returned
the shoe kit to the closet where it was kept. I saw the boys playing in
the den and suggested that they should get ready for "church" on Sunday. The boys disappeared, and I quickly became absorbed in reviewing
sermon notes.

Half an hour later the boys tearfully emerged from the closet where
the shoe kit had been placed. They had covered their white shoes and
large portions of their bodies and clothing with black shoe polish. Simultaneously they lamented, "Daddy, we were trying to get ready for
church like you said, but we messed everything up. We need help." I felt
that they were honestly trying to be obedient. They were following my
orders the best they knew how. However, they had made a colossal mess
of things. How was I to respond to their petition for help? After a brief
subdued chuckle, I responded to their need. I was glad they came to
me and registered their desire for my help, thus indicating their dependence upon me.

The Heavenly Father often sees His children mess things up in a
colossal fashion. Surely, He delights to have them come to Him voic-
ing their weaknesses and inabilities and making their petitions for help
known. Jesus said, "If you then, being evil, know how to give good gifts

to your children, how much more will your father who is in heaven give good things to those who ask him?" (Mt 7:11).

Joseph Scriven, who wrote the words to the hymn "What a Friend We Have in Jesus," was engaged to a beautiful girl who drowned on the eve of their wedding. In his life Joseph Scriven was acquainted with sadness and grief. He wrote the hymn in an attempt to comfort his mother who was gravely ill. The hymn emphasizes the plight that is experienced when one does not make one's requests known to God.

> Oh, what peace we often forfeit,
> Oh, what needless pain we bear,
> All because we do not carry
> Everything to God in prayer!

3. The Prayer of Intercession

The second plateau of prayer is intercession. At this level of prayer, the believer loses all sight of self and prays exclusively for others. At this plateau of prayer, the saint of God has the opportunity to exercise his priesthood in a most meaningful way. This is where he has the privilege and the responsibility of representing man to God.

The word intercede means "to intervene between parties with a view to reconciling differences." An intercessor, therefore, is one who stands in the gap between Holy God and sinful man to plead the case of those separated from God. This is precisely what Jesus, whoever lives to make intercession for us, is doing now. The Bible says, "For Christ has not entered into the holy places made with hands, which are the copies of the true; but into heaven itself, now to appear in the presence of God for us" (Heb 9:24).

Moses truly was one of the greatest intercessors in the Bible. While Moses was in communion with God on Mount Sinai, the rebellious Israelites enticed Aaron to make a golden calf. They sang and danced before the calf and made an idol of it. God's anger was kindled against this open apostasy and idolatry. Moses prayed that God's wrath would be averted and that the people would be forgiven. Hear his selfless prayer of intercession: "Moses returned to the Lord and said, 'Oh, these people have committed a great sin, and have made themselves a god of goldı Yet now, if You will forgive their sin— but if not, I pray blot me out of Your book which You have written" (Ex 32:31-32).

Another example of selfless intercession is found in the plaintive appeal of the apostle Paul for the salvation of the people of Israel. He prayed, "I tell the truth in Christ, I am not lying, my conscience also bearing me witness in the Holy Spirit, that I have great sorrow and continual grief in my heart. For I could wish that I myself were ac-cursed from Christ for my brethren, my countrymen according to the flesh" (Rm 9:1-3). The word "accursed" comes from the word *anathema*. The apostle was indicating that he would forfeit his own communion with Christ on behalf of his countrymen, if in so doing the result would be their salvation. What self-abnegation is expressed by Paul in this prayer! What compassion! He continued to express his concern by say-ing, "Brethren, my heart's desire and prayer to God for Israel is that they may be saved" (Rm 10:1).

If the believer-priest is to rightly assume the responsibility of the New Testament priesthood, he must with a holy intensity become con-cerned for others. Anything else or anything less is to prostitute the of-fice of the priesthood.

Samuel became one of the greatest leaders—a judge, a prophet, and a priest—in the Old Testament. In recognition of his role as an interces-sor, Samuel said, "Moreover, as for me, far be it from me that I should sin against the Lord in ceasing to pray for you" (1 Sm 12:23).

Intercession must not be limited to prayers of concern for the sal-vation of the unredeemed. The believer-priest has the responsibility to pray for "all the saints" (Eph 6:18), "for all who are in authority" (1 Tm 2:2), for those who are sick (Jas 5:14-15), and, indeed, "for all men" (1 Tm 2:1).

4. The Prayer of Communion

The prayer of petition is basically a request for God's help or God's provision in meeting personal needs. It is the first plateau one reaches in climbing the mountain of prayer. The second plateau is the prayer of intercession. In this prayer the focus is upon the needs, the welfare and the blessing of others. But in the prayer of communion the focus is primarily and fundamentally seeking God's fellowship. In this plateau the child of God, having experienced the love of God, responds to that love. He opens the alabaster box of his heart's adoration and pours it out on the feet of the Lord at the throne of grace.

The story is told of the minister who had been inundated with pastoral duties all week. He found himself in his study in the pastorium on Saturday evening poring over his books, preparing his message for the next morning (indeed, there is no inspiration for a preacher like a sinking sun on a Saturday night).

In the midst of a moment of intense concentration on his text, the pastor's seventeen-year-old son bounded into the study. With a glad hand for Dad and a cheery appeal, he inquired, "Hey, Dad, how about allowing me to borrow the car tonight? I've got a date with the prettiest girl in school."

A bit chagrined, the weary father reached in his pocket and reluctantly handed his automobile keys over to his teenage son. In time the dear father was absorbed in his study once again.

The contemplative meditation of the man of God was suddenly interrupted a second time as his adolescent daughter entered the study with two friends. "Dearest Daddy," she said, "could you give me a few dollars? We are going to get a milk shake at the drugstore down the street." The frustrated father grunted a halfhearted approval and gave his daughter the money.

Once again, the pastor regained his thought pattern and began to write out what he thought was a pungent point for his sermon. At the very instant of his greatest inspiration, his four-year-old came bursting into the study, dressed in her pink pajamas. She walked up to his chair and began tugging at his shirt sleeve. In total exasperation the father turned to his youngest child and curtly asked, "Now, what do you want?"

The little girl proceeded to climb up in her father's lap and said, "Daddy, I don't want anything. I just came to love you a little bit."

Sometimes the believer needs to set aside his petitions and be motivated only by the desire to have fellowship with the Father. There are times when the child of God simply needs to crawl up into the Father's lap and love Him a little bit.

As a general rule, prayer is a one-sided conversation. The child does all the talking and the Father does all the listening. The believer gives little or no time for the Heavenly Father to communicate His will in the time of prayer. Therefore, pray before an open Bible. Speak to God. Allow God's Word to speak to you. Prayer should be a dialogue, not a monologue.

In Exodus 33, God and Moses had a time of communion. The Bible says, "The Lord spoke to Moses face to face, as a man speaks to his friend" (v. 11). This experience of fellowship with God on Mount Sinai lasted forty days and forty nights. Moses' communion with God consisted of praying, listening, praising, and worshiping.

At the conclusion of this time of fellowship with God, Moses stood before the children of Israel and "gave them as commandments all that the Lord had spoken with him on Mount Sinai" (Ex 34:32). However, the experience of communion with God had so affected Moses that his face glistened with the light of the glory of God. He had to put a veil over his face before he could address the congregation of Israel.

One of the primary reasons I consider this the highest level of prayer is because it is this prayer that meets one of the requirements for revival. In 2 Chronicles 7:14 God says, "If My people who are called by My name will humble themselves, and pray and seek my face, and turn from their wicked ways, then will I hear from heaven, and will forgive their sin and will heal their land."

Please notice that God does not request here that we seek His hand. That is what we seek when we pray the prayer of petition. In the prayer of communion, we seek His face. In the prayer of intercession we pray for others, but in the prayer of communion, we are simply seeking God and we have no other desire than entering into His presence, loving Him, and cultivating the intimate relationship He desires to have with us. When we do that we have met one of the crucial conditions for genuine, heaven sent revival in our life and potentially in the lives of countless others.

Dwelling in the presence of the Lord will give the saint of God a glowing countenance and the desire for an even more personal, profound, cherished walk with Him. This is the third plateau as we climb up the mountain of prayer.

III. THE POWER OF PRAYER

God moves and responds to the prayers of His people. E. M. Bounds wrote, "Prayer projects faith on God, and God on the world. Only God can move mountains, but faith and prayer move God."[1] When one depends upon promotion, one gets what promotion can do. When one depends upon oratory, one gets what oratory can do. When one depends upon organization, one gets what organization can do. But when one depends upon prayer, one gets what omnipotent God can do.

1. Prayer Results in the Regeneration of the Lost

The believer-priest has the responsibility of praying for the lost. The Bible urges intercessory prayer for those who are outside the fold of God. Indeed, it is upon the wings of prayer that souls are born into the kingdom of God.

People are lost because of the wiles and the manipulative schemes of the devil. Satan appeals to the fleshly nature of man, tempts him to sin, and seeks to hold him captive by his powers of darkness. The devil will contend with any endeavor designed to win souls to faith in Christ. Successful evangelism employs a strategy for binding the stronghold of Satan in the life of the unbeliever. Jesus said, "No one can enter a strong man's house and plunder his goods, unless he first binds the strong man.

And then he will plunder his house" (Mk 3:27). The strong man is none other than Satan himself. His goods are the souls of men.

In order to enter Satan's domain and contest him for the souls of men, the believer-priest must bind him through prayer. Only as Satan is bound does the soulwinner have the freedom to release the captives from the domain of the devil. If night after night the believer baptizes his bedside with the briny tears of intercession for the lost, he can live each day in anticipation of a glorious harvest of souls. Going on an evangelism assignment without praying is like a baseball player trying to hit a home run without swinging a bat. It would be far better to pray and not go than to go and not pray.

On the cross Jesus prayed for the lost, those who were responsible for His crucifixion. His first statement from the cross was the prayer, "Father, forgive them, for they do not know what they do" (Lk 23:34). In essence, Jesus Christ prayed for their redemption. The popular belief is that many of them were saved in the weeks and months that followed. Thus, the prayer of Jesus from the cross surely contributed to the salvation of many on the Day of Pentecost.

There were three thousand saved on the Day of Pentecost (Ac 2:41). In Acts 6:7, the Word of God states that "the number of disciples multiplied greatly in Jerusalem, and a great many of the priests were obedient to the faith."

Truly, prayer will reach down into the places of degradation and debauchery and take hold of those who seem to be lost beyond all hope of redemption. Prayer extends even beyond the reach of man's witness to stir the slumbering souls of the unregenerate. Through the faithful intercession of God's saints, vile and wicked men are lifted up from the cesspools of society and made fit for the city of God.

2. Prayer Produces Empowerment for Service

Every believer has the privilege of being endued with the power of God for Christian service. Jesus did not want His disciples to attempt the divine work without the divine power. He told them, "Tarry in the city of Jerusalem until you are endued with power from on high" (Lk 24:49).

Surely the disciples remonstrated with Jesus. They could see the desperation written on the faces of the multitudes. They could hear the crying of the sick and the sorrowful. They could smell the stench of deprivation and want. They could sense the hopelessness of those who were sinking in sin. The urgency of the hour must have caused their spirits to resist the principle of tarrying. However, Jesus insisted that their tarrying was a requisite to their being endued with divine power.

What was this matter of tarrying? What was it that the disciples did for those ten days in that upper room in Jerusalem before the advent of the Holy Spirit? Those days must have included prayer, meditation, confession, consecration, and surrender. Those disciples did not while away those crucial hours in idle chatter and parlor games. They got right with God. They reconciled every relationship. They exchanged their weakness for God's strength. Through communion with God in prayer, they had a heartwarming. Then the Holy Spirit came upon them, and they left that upper room to change their world for Christ.

Empowered by the Holy Spirit through prayer, the early disciples became effective in their work and in their witness. The church grew phenomenally. By the seventeenth chapter of Acts, those early disciples were referred to as those who "turned the world upside down" (v. 6). By the 19th chapter of Acts, those first-century Christians had pressed themselves against every door in Asia Minor with the result that within the space of two years "all who dwelt in Asia heard the word of the Lord Jesus, both Jews and Greeks" (v. 10). Because they tarried in prayer, they were energized and motivated by the Holy Spirit. The result was the evangelization of the world.

The same power that aided the early Christians is available to believers today. The power of the Holy Spirit is a power over all other distinctions of power. The apostle Paul must have known that power because after years of ministry he wrote, "Now thanks be unto God who always leads us in triumph in Christ, and through us diffuses the fragrance of His knowledge in every place" (2 Cor 2:14). This was obviously the experience of Robert Murray McCheyne, who said, "Remember Jesus for us is all our righteousness before a Holy God. Jesus in us is all our strength in an ungodly world."[2] This strength is appropriated to the ministry of the saint through prayer.

History records the tremendous response Jonathan Edwards had to his sermon "Sinners in the Hands of an Angry God." Though he meticulously read the manuscript of his sermon word for word, the convicting power of God fell upon that New England congregation that day. Sinners were converted and lives were dramatically changed. The untold story is that Jonathan Edwards not only had prepared the message to deliver but also had prepared himself to deliver the message. He had not eaten or slept for three days and nights. He begged God for heavenly unction and power. When he entered the pulpit that day, the congregation saw a man who had been gazing into the face of God.

Prayer can produce empowerment for service. The apostle Paul underscored his confidence in this principle when he requested of the Christians of Thessalonica: "Finally, brethren, pray for us, that the word of the Lord may run swiftly and be glorified" (2 Thes 3:1).

3. Prayer Results in Revival in the Church

A revival or a funeral? This is the issue facing many churches today. Unfortunately, there are few churches in genuine revived because there are few churches really committed to prayer. R. A. Torrey declared:

> Time and time again the church has seemed to be on the verge of utter shipwreck; but just then God has sent a great revival and saved it. If you will study the history of revivals, you will find that every real revival in the church has been the result of prayer. There have been revivals without much preaching; there have been revivals with absolutely no organization; but there has never been a mighty revival without mighty prayer.[2]

The biblical prescription for revival is found in 2 Chronicles 7:14: "If My people who are called by My name will humble themselves, and pray, and seek My face, and turn from their wicked ways, then I will hear from heaven, and will forgive their sin, and will heal their land."

The indispensable ingredient of revival is the kind of prayer that seeks the face of God as mentioned earlier in this chapter. What a colossal difference it would make in the church if the believer-priest would exercise his privilege of entering into the presence of God and establishing that intimacy.

In the latter part of the last century I went to Korea and discovered that many of their churches were vibrant, growing, and glowing. They pulsated with life. Why? I discovered that believers were exercising their priestly privilege of prayer. In the early hours of the day the Korean Christians gathered to their churches for prayer. Their prayer meetings were not hit-and-miss attempts to get in touch with God. It was obvious that they knew how to communicate with the Heavenly Father. The only thing that stands between the revived churches of Korea in that day and the lethargic churches of America today are believer-priests who have not disciplined themselves to commune with God until their lives are expressions of an intimacy with Him. The Bible plainly states that "the effective, fervent prayer of a righteous man avails much" (Jas 5:16).

When believer-priests understand that there is power to regenerate the lost, to empower every work for Jesus, and to revive the church, a new day will dawn for the cause of Christ in the land. To have the privilege and decline the responsibility is hypocrisy at its worst!

Notes

1. Edward M. Bounds, *The Necessity of Prayer* (Grand Rapids: Baker Book House, 1976), p. 10.

2. http://www.mcheyne.info/life.php

3. R. A. Torrey, *The Power of Prayer* (Grand Rapids: Zondervan Publishing House, 1971), p. 43.

9

The Believer-Priest and Pastoral Authority (Hebrews 13:7,17; 1 Peter 5:1-4)

From time to time in evangelical circles there is a renewed emphasis upon the congregational involvement in ministry. This is an emphasis that should be welcomed in every church by both the pew and the pulpit. For too many years church members depended upon a professional clergy to carry on the Lord's work. On the other hand, many pastors have been remiss in "the perfecting of the saints for the work of the ministry." Today, there are many "performance or entertainment driven" churches.

Marsha West in an article posted by the *Stand Up for the Truth* website writes: "No question, we are a culture that loves to be entertained. Even churches have caught on to the public's desire for 24/7 entertainment. As a consequence, a large number of evangelical churches are now driven by a need to fulfill this desire in their congregants. And what better way to pack the house in enormous auditoriums than to offer a 90-minute stage show enhanced with state-of-the-art sound, lighting and video systems.

To help spice up worship, a team of want-to-be actors treat the audience to a short skit that ties in with the message (sermon). As the lights dim and the actors scurry off stage, a hip cool pastor wearing skinny jeans, a logo T-shirt, and a five o'clock shadow ambles out to preach the "new" Good News. Hip cool pastors aren't your average run of the mill ministers. Some of these guys are genuine entertainers loaded with talent! They're bona fide performers. True showmen. And some of them are comics! In fact, most hip cool pastors could walk off the church stage onto a Las Vegas stage and feel right at home. No really, they're that good!¹

The church functions at its best when every member is exercising his or her spiritual gift "for the equipping of the saints" (Eph 4:12). Elton Trueblood, in his book *Your Other Vocation*, wrote, "If we should take lay-religion seriously as was done in the early Christian church, the dull picture presented by so many contemporary churches would be radically altered [...] Pastors would not be performing while others watched, but helping to stir up the ministry of the ordinary members."²

Jesus Christ has His greatest impact upon the world when Christians collectively exert their influence right where they are—in the neighborhood and in the marketplace, day in and day out. As the people of God become the church militant and lift up the standard of Christ aggressively in the land, society is infected with a contagious witness of the power of the living God. It is high time for every believer to understand that he is an ambassador for Christ on a divine mission. Every saint needs to report for duty, and no child of God should be AWOL.

Those responsible for stirring up church members and motivating them to become involved are to be saluted. The pastor and parishioner need to join hands and hearts in Christian ministry. However, the coining of phrases such as "claity" (derived from clergy and laity) may militate against the biblical principle of pastoral authority. In this chapter consideration will be given to the difference between intrinsic worth and functional role as may be applicable to the believer-priest and pastoral authority.

I. THE AUTHORITY OF THE PASTOR

The Bible clearly teaches pastoral authority. Authority given, however, is often authority abused. In a message preached at Southeastern Baptist Theological Seminary in Wake Forest, North Carolina, emphasizing "The Minister as Servant," Chevis F. Horne proclaimed: "The wrong use of power can be evil, but it is especially demonic in the hands of religious people. This is true because they think they are doing the will of God. This blinds them to the evil they are doing."[3] Although Reverend Horne's words are true, sometimes statements are made that deemphasize the importance of the pastor as the spiritual leader of the local church. Occasionally pastoral authority may be abused, but that does not justify the denigration of the principle.

In Paul's day the Lord's Supper was abused in Corinth, but the observance of the ordinance was not discontinued. Careful attention must be given so that the baby is not thrown out with the bathwater. If the church fails to honor the pastor as the spiritual leader of the church, it is showing evidence of rebellion against God's design for an orderly fellowship.

1. The Order Which God Has Designed

Every believer is of equal worth in God's sight. "There is neither Jew nor Greek, there is neither slave nor free, there is neither male nor female: for you are all one in Christ Jesus" (Gal 3:28). The ground is level at the foot of the cross. There is no preferential treatment for male over female, the free man over the incarcerated man, or Jew over Gentile. There is oneness, harmony, and equity in Christ Jesus.

For example, although Jesus is referred to as the second person of the Godhead, that does not mean He is inferior to the Father. He was fully

God and fully man. He could say, "I and My Father are one" (Jn 10:30); but when it came to functional roles, Jesus prayed, "Father, if it is Your will, take this cup away from Me; nevertheless, not My will, but Yours, be done" (Lk 22:42). In the area of intrinsic worth there was equality, but in the area of functional roles there was a difference—even in the Godhead. Paul, under the inspiration of the Holy Spirit, wrote, "The head of every man is Christ, the head of woman is man; and the head of Christ is God" (1 Cor 11:3).

During the midst of the Conservative Resurgence among Southern Baptists in the early 1980s moderate leaders were on a crusade to affirm women for all and any kind of ministerial role by emphasizing what they called the "indiscrimination of gifts." Roy Honeycutt, president of Southern Baptist Theological Seminary during those tumultuous days, wrote a pamphlet entitled "Affirming Women in Ministry". He stated, "Affirming women in ministry is faithful to the Bible, and to our consistent determination to reflect an authentic biblical theology. . . . Concerning gifts for women, some may seek to limit Paul's list of gifts to men simply because the New Testament commonly uses the third person masculine pronoun "he." But God's Spirit is indiscriminate in His distribution of spiritual gifts."

About the same time Dr. Honeycutt wrote his booklet, Southeastern Baptist Theological Seminary had a "Celebration of the New Humanity" in their chapel service. In addition to Nancy Unterzuber bringing the message there was a liturgy adapted from a reading included in Sistercelebrations: Nine Worship Experiences. The female liturgist declared, "We as women are strong. We as women are powerful. We as women can do things. We need to be more in touch with our strength, our power, and our capabilities. We need to be free to be ourselves. We need not stifle our God-given talents.

The male liturgists replied, "When you are free, then we are freer. We don't have to prove our manliness. We don't have to prove our 'natural superiority.' We don't have to claim anything. We need to be more in touch with our tears. We need to be free to be ourselves. We need to discard our 'masculine role' and discover who we really are."

Then everyone responded: "We reject the notion that one sex should build bridges and the other keep the home. We reject the idea of 'proper roles' for roles belong to the realm of law, and freedom belongs to the gospel. We believe the words of the New Testament that in God's time and place there is no male and female, no mankind or womankind, no manhood or womanhood, but simply humanhood, simply God's people. We can and will be more human. We will find ways of being men and women together."[4]

It is unwise to blur the God-given distinction between men and women. Indeed, God created men and women as equals in terms of value and significance, but the Bible makes it clear that they have uniquely different functioning roles in the home and in the church.

Several years ago, my wife and I were on a vacation in New England with my brother and his wife. On a Sunday we were in Kennebunkport, Maine and on our way to see former president George H. W. Bush's compound we drove along the Atlantic coast and passed by the Village Baptist Church. I noticed that Reverend Pat Batten's name was on the church sign and I thought, "Good, we can come back and listen to Brother Patrick's sermon this morning." So, on the way back from seeing the Bush vacation home beautifully situated on the rugged Atlantic coast, we stopped at the quaint little church for our worship experience.

We were warmly greeted at the front door of the church and entered the small, but welcoming sanctuary. We sat in quiet anticipation of the worship service. After the organ prelude the robed minister walked into the pulpit, but it was not Brother Patrick. It was Sister Patricia! When the music, the prayers and the offertory ended Reverend Patricia Batten delivered the message. There is something within me that almost wants to say that the message was boring and ineffective, but that was not the case at all. She delivered an expository message that was beautifully crafted, true to the Word of God and presented with clarity and passion.

After five years as pastor of the Village Baptist Church, which is affiliated with the American Baptist Convention, Dr. Batten became a part of the faculty of Gordon - Conwell Theological Seminary where she serves as the Ranked Adjunct Professor of Preaching. On her website she professes to "find great pleasure in teaching soon-to-be pastors how to preach expository sermons." She also continues to maintain an active preaching ministry. While, Dr. Batten is a personable, talented, experienced communicator, is she ministering within the parameters or constraints of God's Word? This is a question that is inextricably entangled in thorny brambles and scratchy briars, but my contention is that she is not. When the Apostle Paul writes his first epistle to Timothy, his son in the ministry, he states, "Let a woman learn in silence with all submission. And do not permit a woman to teach or to have authority over a man, but to be in silence" (I Tm 2:11-12). There is absolutely no debate whatsoever that this biblical injunction expressly forbids women from holding the principle position of authoritative doctrinal teaching in the Ephesian church. Since God's Word is immutable it is correct to contend that women should not "wear" the mantle of doctrinal authority in the local church today.

Two different paradigms concerning the roles of men and women have once again gained much attention in the church in recent years. While complementarianism has been the view traditionally embraced by evangelicals from time immemorial, the concept of egalitarianism has begun to gain favor among many denominations in recent years. Complementarianism is the theological view that although men and women are created equal in their being and personhood, they are created to complement each other via different roles in life and in the church. This view emphasizes that women are equal to men in intrinsic worth, but have different functional roles. This view is consistent with Holy Scripture and embraced by conservative Baptists. While we may hold to the complementarian understanding of Scripture, many of us would express concern about those who misuse or abuse it.

The second paradigm is egalitarianism, which is the view that men and women are designed by their Creator to have no gender-limitations of what functions or roles each can fulfill in the home, the church and society. The egalitarian view is that there are no roles or responsibilities that uniquely fall to the male and no imitations of what functions the female can fulfill in the home, the church and the society. According to this view, women as well as men can serve as pastors, elders, and deacons. It would appear that egalitarians take scripture verses like Galatians 3:28 and contend that gifts trump gender.

So, while egalitarians seem to adhere to the infallibility of the Bible, they interpret it to conform to their doctrinal position. Others hold to this view because they have a desire to champion the social justice movement or because they are a part of the "Woke Church".

Tim Challis, author and co-founder of Cruciform Press, explained why he is committed to the complementarian view in his blog, titled, "Why I am Not an Egalitarian." He wrote,

> "The complexity of words like ezer (Hebrew word for helpmate) and phrases like "mutual submission" are far more easily resolved by complementarians than "I do not permit a woman to teach or to have authority over a man" is for egalitarians. Paul's appeals to Adam's priority in the order of creation, the distinct male focus in the qualifications of an (pastor), the extended teaching on marriage in Ephesians 5, the deep mystery and metaphor within marriage—all of these provide challenges to the egalitarian position that I consider insurmountable."[5]

The order which God has designed for the home is consistent with the order he has for the church. The Bible declares that "the husband is head of the wife" and the wives are to be in subjection "to their own husbands in everything" (Eph 5:23-24). These words do not in any way suggest that a woman is inferior to a man. There is equal intrinsic worth but differing functional roles.

Likewise, in the home there is a role to which the children must conform. Again, in his Ephesian letter Paul wrote, "Children, obey your parents in the Lord: for this is right" (Eph 6:1). Frequently, mothers wonder why they must contend with rebellious children. Often that struggle occurs because of their own resistance to the authority of their husband. The Bible teaches that when one submits to the authority over him/her, that person can more readily expect submission from those who are under him/her (Mt 8:9). Every family member: father, mother, teenager, and thumb-sucking infant are of the same created worth. However, God's design of differing roles is for order in the home. Wherever these roles are not honored, there is agony in the family.

There is also a divinely designed order for society. The Word of God speaks of "kings, and all who are in authority" (1Tm 2:2). The further declaration of Scripture is, "Let every soul be subject to the governing authorities" (Rm 13:1). When there is submission to and intercession for "the authorities" in government, there is the prospect of leading "a quiet and peaceable life" (1 Tm 2:2).

In terms of intrinsic worth, every citizen is as important as the president, but, once again, there is a difference in functional roles. When authority is resisted in society, there is anarchy. Since "God is not the author of confusion but of peace" (1 Cor 14:33), He has also established an order for the church. The writer of Hebrews declared:

> Remember those who rule over you, who have spoken the word of God to you: whose faith follow, considering the outcome of their conduct . . . Obey those who rule over you, and be submissive, for they watch out for your souls, as those who must give account. Let them do so with joy and not with grief: for that would be unprofitable for you (Heb 13:7,17).

These verses enjoin submission to those "who have spoken unto you the word of God" and those who "watch for your souls." Herein is God's design for the pastor to be the spiritual leader of the local church. The validity of this principle is underscored in 1 Peter 5:1-4. When authority is resisted in the home, there is agony. When authority is resisted in society, there is anarchy. When authority is resisted in the church, there is adversity.

2. The Oversight Which God Has Decreed

Just as many husbands have abdicated the role of spiritual leader in the home, many pastors have abdicated their rightful role of spiritual leader in the church. It elicits Satan's glee to see a pastor relinquish his role as the spiritual leader of the church. The devil is doubly gratified when he sees the church being led by the deacons or by some bureaucracy because he knows that violates scriptural principles.

Baptist polity through the years has affirmed two scriptural offices in the New Testament: pastor and deacon (Phil 1:1). The 2000 Baptist Faith and Message underscores this principle in Article VI with these words: "Its scriptural officers are pastors and deacons."

The Word of God says the elders or pastors are "to feed the flock of God ... taking the oversight thereof" (1 Pt 5:2, KJV). The phrase "taking the oversight" comes from the Greek word episkopountes and means "to perform the duties of one who oversees." There is always the danger of a pastor aspiring to become a superstar shepherd. Some have become tyrants. Others think of themselves as vicars of Christ. Occasionally a pastor may have some kind of messiah complex. These cases are the rare exceptions to the norm.

Indeed, there are far more pastors who do not relish the role of authority. Many others accept the role of leadership, not because it is enticing, but because it is according to God's design. Thankfully, a growing number of churches are conforming to the scriptural principle of pastoral authority. They have been taught the Word of God and have submitted to its precepts. The pastor offers loving leadership, and the people rejoice to have it so.

John MacArthur, pastor of the Grace Community Church in Panorama City, California, wrote:

> In many churches today the congregation rules the leaders. This sort of government is foreign to the New Testament. Church leaders are not to be tyrants because they do not rule for themselves, but for God [...] It is the right of

such men, under God and in meekness and humility to determine the direction of the church, to preside over it, to teach the Word in it, to reprove, rebuke, and exhort [...] Pastors . . . are undershepherds, who serve under the "Chief Shepherd."[6]

To provide spiritual leadership for a local body of believers is an awesome responsibility. A pastor might be morally pure, doctrinally sound, oratorically brilliant, and yet very ineffective as a leader.

The Bible says, "Where there is no vision the people perish" (Prv 29:18, KJV). An effective leader is a man of vision. A pastor might want to lead and, yet, have no sense of direction. In reality, vision is seeing what ought to be done, what can be done, and a way to do it. Many churches suffer from visionless leadership. Countless pastors do not live in close enough communion with God to have a vision for the church. Other pastors refuse to be the spiritual authority God has ordained them to be; thus, the local assembly of believers suffers because no church will rise above its leadership.

The faithful pastor who provides direction for the church as the spiritual authority becomes a prime target for Satanic attack. His every move is subject to criticism. His leadership is questioned. His decisions are second guessed. His motives are suspect. This divinely delegated role is not for the spiritually weak or fainthearted. The role of pastor is for God-called men who know the Lord, live in constant contact with Him, and dare to communicate His will to the people.

3. The Obedience Which God Has Demanded

The writer of Hebrews urged submission to pastoral authority when he declared, "Obey those who rule over you, and be submissive" (Heb 13:17). The human spirit rebels against submission, but God's order for the church is that the pastor provides the leadership, and church members provide the appropriate response to that leadership. They are of equal intrinsic worth, but in the economy of God their functional roles are different.

In his book *Enemy in the Pew*, Daniel D. Walker described five kinds of relationships or attitudes church members have toward their pastors. First, he suggests that there are those who tend to worship the pastor. These are the idolaters. They put the clergy on a pedestal and offer reverence and adoration in an unrealistic fashion. Some clergymen actually solicit this kind of response. They should have the attitude of Peter when Cornelius fell at his feet and worshiped him. The Bible says, "But Peter lifted him up, saying, Stand up; I myself am also a man" (Ac 10:26).

Walker proposed that the second type of church member is the patron. People with a patronizing attitude have ulterior motives. Oftentimes they use their wealth or influence to buy the pastor's friendship or exert pressure on him for some particular reason. The pastor who invites or allows such patronization may ultimately find himself much like the hireling Jesus warned against (Jn 10:12-13).

Another attitude reflected by some church members toward the clergy is that of critic. Constructive counsel, born out of prayer and offered in love, should be welcomed by the minister. However, most criticism, at best, is the expression of some trivial personal bias, or, at worst, a vicious attack designed to destroy. Walker stated that most criticism "expresses a feeling of superiority. It carries the assumption that the layman is an adequate judge of what a preacher should be. [...] For such a layman the preacher is not a man of God whose words are to be heeded, but an employee of the congregation whose work is to be perfected."[7]

The fourth attitude church members may take toward their pastor is that of an enemy. There are people in certain churches who have set themselves up to "protect" the church against any kind of spiritual leader. They have taken great pride in being able to maintain control of the local assembly. Those who are antagonistic toward the pastor may help him improve his prayer life, but they may destroy his ministry, his health and bring dissension into the church. Those who take potshots at the preacher place themselves in a precarious spiritual position, for

God declared, "Do not touch My anointed ones, and do My prophets no harm" (Ps 105:15).

Walker also suggested that church members sometime take the attitude of competitor in relating to the pastor. They envy the position of leadership held by the pastor and often contend to wrest him from that role of authority. There are church people who are content to "let the minister be the church's voice if they can function as its brain."[8] However, it is not the place of the membership to compete with the pastor, but to complement him in the work of the ministry.

The pastor should love his flock, care for them, seek their counsel and assistance, gently lead them to know and do the will of God, and always endeavor "to keep the unity of the Spirit in the bond of peace" (Eph 4:3). Church members should submit to the authority of the pastor by their faithful "followship."

II. THE ACTIVITY OF THE PASTOR

The pastor who provides effective leadership and wears well the role of authority is the pastor whose activity and demeanor conform to the will and way of God. A backslidden preacher could scarcely expect the unqualified submission of his congregation. The proper lifestyle and activity of the pastor is carefully outlined in 1 Peter 5.

1. Exemplify the Master

Peter wrote that pastors have the responsibility of "being examples to the flock" (1 Pt 5:3, NIV). In this passage the word "example" is *tupos* which means to make a mark by striking a blow. It is the same word used in John 20:25 (NIV) when Thomas said, "Unless I see the nail marks in his hands...I will not believe." The pastor is to make a good and godly mark or imprint upon the lives of his people. He is not to present himself as one who has achieved perfection. He is to be an example of one who has denied himself; one who is taking up his cross daily; and one who is consciously allowing Jesus to be the Lord of his life.

Each pastor should so live that he could say with Paul, "Imitate me, just as I also imitate Christ" (1 Cor 11:1). The Greek word for imitate is *mimetes* from which the word mimic comes. Paul urged the Corinthian church to mimic or imitate him because he was imitating Christ. When Paul wrote Timothy, he emphasized the importance of the young preacher's being "an example [*tupos*] to the believers in word, in conduct, in love, in spirit, in faith, in purity" (1 Tm 4:12).

Unfortunately, many ministers fail to develop their own personal relationship to God, fall into sin, and thus diminish or forfeit their effectiveness as a spiritual leader. However, when the man of God spends time alone with God, he sees the promises of the Father glow with a heavenly light. The warnings of Scripture loom over the horizon like frightening shadows. The comforts of God's Word are distilled like the dew upon a parched land. In that trysting place, sin is revealed in its ugliness in the light of God's countenance. In that quiet place Christ is revealed in ravishing beauty. Heaven and earth are brought into sharp focus. Temptations are resisted and faith is triumphant. The application of the blood is felt in fresh, renewing power. There the Holy Spirit anoints and qualifies for ministry, for preaching, for leadership. The more time the pastor spends alone with God, the more he becomes like the Master and the more he becomes an example to the flock.

Napoleon said, "The greatest immorality is for a man to occupy a place that he cannot fill." No man can fill the role of pastor unless he is daily seeking to conform to the image of Christ and thus becoming an example to the people God has entrusted to his care.

2. Expound the Message

The faithful pastor not only will exemplify the Master but also will expound the message. Peter, exhorting the elders (pastors), wrote, "Feed the flock of God which is among you" (1 Pt 5:2, KJV). The word "feed" comes from the Greek word *poimaino* which means "to shepherd." It means to tend, protect, guide, love, pray for, and feed the flock of God. One pastor said, "My problem is not that of feeding the flock, but getting them hungry enough to want to be fed." That problem seems to persist in many churches. The people seem to have little appetite for the things of God. There is little capacity for spiritual food. Pray that the people of our churches would have hungry hearts. Pray that they will cry out with the psalmist, "As the deer pants after the water brooks, so pants my soul after You, O God" (Ps 42:1). "O God, You are my God; early will I seek You: my soul thirsts for You, my flesh longs for You in a dry and thirsty land, where there is no water. So, I have looked for You in the sanctuary, to see Your power and Your glory" (Ps 63:1-2). This should be the heart cry of the people of God, but, alas, a spirit of apathy often prevails.

Nevertheless, the shepherd is to expound the message, to feed the sheep. He must "preach the word! Be ready in season and out of season" (2 Tm 4:2). He must expound the message when it's convenient and when it's not convenient; when it is expedient and when it is not expedient; when they will listen and when they are dull of hearing.

If the shepherd is to feed the flock of God, he must understand the necessity of being divinely anointed by the Holy Spirit. In writing to the church of Thessalonica, Paul avowed, "For our gospel did not come to you in word only, but also in power, and in the Holy Spirit" (1 Thes 1:5). In preaching, the man of God must remember that the important thing is not the clever outline or the ingenious alliteration or the perceptive illustrations or the knowledge demonstrated. The important thing is the anointing of the Holy Spirit. Preaching without the power of the Holy Spirit is but so much hot air.

The pastor may stand behind the pulpit and preach truth, but only the Holy Spirit can impart truth. What the pulpits of the land need today is not an explanation of the power of God, but a demonstration of the power of God. Only as the man of God proclaims the truth of God in the power of God to the people of God will they rightly be fed.

3. Equip the Members

A significant portion of the pastor's ministry should be directed toward the equipping of the members. To the church in Ephesus Paul wrote, "And He gave some to be apostles; some prophets, and some evangelists; and some pastors and teachers, for the equipping of the saints for the work of the ministry" (Eph 4:11-12). The Greek word for "equipping" is *katartismas* which means "fitting or preparing fully."

Today churches are plagued with a "spectator Christianity." Occasionally we hear someone say, "We hired us a preacher. Let him do the work." That concept is not scriptural. It is not the business of the pastor to do the work of the ministry. The work of the pastor is to equip his people to do the work of the ministry. The best pastor-equippers are not those who teach by precept only, but who teach by example as well. How beautiful to behold the church where the pastor and the people work in harmony and cooperation to advance the kingdom enterprise.

Some things are better caught than taught. If the pastor fails to inspire the saints by his own devotional life, his own personal walk with God, his own self-discipline, his own work ethic, there is little inspiration for the member to fulfill "the work of the ministry."

Some years ago, Dr. E. V. Hill, then the dynamic pastor in the Watts area of Los Angeles, spoke of the sixty-two separate ministering groups in his church. He emphasized the importance of every member being a minister. So many people get lost out on the periphery of the church because they have never been motivated to get involved or equipped to be a ministering member.

Three things happen when the pastor equips the members to minister. First, when every member is involved in service it will eliminate complainers. The football player who always has to sit on the bench and who never gets to play in the games will generally begin to murmur and complain. He will say, "The coach is unfair. He is biased. I could play better than anyone on the first team. The quarterback is a klutz. We would have won if I had been in the game."

Occasionally, the bench-sitter will even resort to favoring his team's opponent. However, those who participate in the game are so occupied with blocking, tackling, kicking, running, and all of the rudiments of the game they have no time nor desire to complain. The equipped and involved church member is rarely critical.

Every member ministering not only eliminates complainers but results in the edification of the church. The church is the body of Christ. Christ is the head of this body. Every member is part and parcel of the body. When every member is functioning according to his capacity or spiritual gift the body operates smoothly and efficiently.

Dizzy Dean was an outstanding pitcher on the Saint Louis Cardinals baseball team. One summer day when Dizzy was on the mound for the Cardinals, he threw a pitch which Earl Averill hit back toward the mound. The ball hit Dizzy Dean on his toe and ruined his pitching arm.

"Impossible!" you say?

Here's what happened.

The next time Dizzy pitched he overcompensated for his afflicted toe by overextending his pitching arm and ruined his delivery. He got a sore arm and ultimately had to give up the game because of the damage done to his arm.

Similarly, when one member of the body of Christ does not function properly for whatever reason the whole body is thrown out of kilter. The body of Christ is at its best when all members are fulfilling their divine purpose, operating according to God's will, and complementing the whole. Ministering members edify the church.

Thirdly, ministering members exalt the Creator. The Lord is never honored by believers who are uninvolved and slothful. The child of God is to be an active, positive witness in this world. Jesus said, "You are the light of the world...Let your light so shine before men, that they may see your good works and glorify your Father which is in heaven" (Mt 5:14,16).

The pastor has the solemn responsibility under God of equipping the members, the saints of God, so that his efforts in kingdom service are multiplied by an involved and committed congregation.

4. Examine the Motivations

The faithful pastor will be careful also to spend some of his devotional time in examining the motives that inspire him to serve as an undershepherd. Peter noted that there are pastors who serve "by constraint or compulsion" (1 Pt 5:2). Indeed, there are many who minister not because they feel that it is a liberating joy, but because they feel it is their duty, and quite a burdensome duty at that. They have the dark sensation that they are in prison by their calling to the ministry.

How often a pastor has said, "I would get out of the ministry if there were anything else in the world I thought I could do." Peter implied that some pastors assume their role for the sake of "filthy lucre" (1 Pt 5:2, KJV). The Greek word for "filthy lucre" is *aischrokerdos* and denotes "a grasping, greedy spirit." In most cases there is a minimal amount of material gain to be derived from being the pastor of a local church. However, in many churches the pastor is the center of attention. He has achieved a position of power with a capacity to use his authority for good or evil. He has the privilege of standing before his congregation as a humble servant, to proclaim the unsearchable riches of Christ or perform his monologue and win the applause of his hearers. Some pastors stand in the pulpit to achieve personal recognition, rather than to bring glory to God. Therefore, the pastor must continually examine his motivations for ministry.

Peter insisted that he should serve "willingly" and "of a ready mind" (1 Pt 5:2). Peter may have been reflecting upon the time when, after his denial of Jesus, the resurrected Lord appeared to him by the Sea of Galilee to renew his commission as an apostle. Jesus impressed upon Peter that the greatest motivation for the ministry is not love for the sheep or love for the feeding of sheep, but a love for the Lord of the sheep. If the pastor of the church loves the Lord with all his heart, soul, and strength, he will minister willingly and with a ready mind. His motivation will be pure and God-honoring.

III. THE ACCOUNTABILITY OF THE PASTOR

The writer of Hebrews reminded the undershepherd that the day will come when he "must give account" (Heb 13:17).

1. The Day of Reckoning

Since much is given to the pastor of the church much shall be required of him at the judgment seat of Christ. At the bema, the judgment seat of Christ, every believer will be judged on the basis of his works, to determine the measure of his reward. This judgment is described in 1 Corinthians 3:13-15: "each one's work will become clear; for the Day will declare it, because it will be revealed by fire; and the fire will test each one's work, of what sort it is. If anyone's work which he has built on it endures, he will receive a reward. If anyone's work is burned, he will suffer loss; but he himself will be saved, yet so as through fire."

On this day of reckoning those who have served as the pastors of churches will have their ministry, their messages, and their motivations put to the test by fire. Some will be ashamed when they see many of their good works burned away because they were not born out of a proper motivation.

Some pastors will have it revealed that they were only "hirelings" (Jn 10:12-13). Others will find that they were careless and faithless in the discharge of their ministry. That there is a day of reckoning makes the true shepherd ever vigilant, compassionate, and faithful. As the undershepherd, he understands his responsibility to the Chief Shepherd (1 Pt 5:4). In his private communion with the Father, he reflects upon the condition of the congregation committed to his trust. He lives in anticipation of the day when the Chief Shepherd shall ask, "Where is the flock that was given to you, your beautiful sheep?" (Jer 13:20).

On that day the pastor hopes he will be able to give an account for every soul entrusted to his care. The greatest joy of any undershepherd is to see those who have been entrusted to him grow in the grace and knowledge of the Lord Jesus Christ and produce much fruit. John wrote, "I have no greater joy than to hear that my children walk in truth" (3 Jn 4). Conversely, one of the saddest things that a true pastor can experience is to spend his life in service to others who do not grow, who resist spiritual leadership, and who fail to walk in truth. The flock is to follow the shepherd in such obedience that his accounting at the bema can be "with joy and not with grief" (Heb 13:17).

The church at Corinth was apparently a carnal, refractory fellowship. When Paul thought of the believers there, he could not speak to them "as to spiritual" (1 Cor 3:1). He thought of the Corinthians as being plagued by "envy, strife, and divisions" (v.3). In the mind of Paul this carnal church conjured up images of duplicity (10:21), and perversions of the Lord's Supper (11:28-29), and abuses of spiritual gifts (12:14). They were afflicted with heresies (11:19), and worldliness (2 Cor 6:14-18). Paul, no doubt, trembled with trepidation as he thought about having to give account for the church in Corinth. His report on the condition of Corinth would be given with grief. However, Paul's experience with some of the other churches was evidently more satisfying.

When reflecting upon his experience with the church at Philippi, he positively declared, "I thank my God upon every remembrance of you, always in every prayer of mine making request for you all with joy, for your fellowship in the gospel from the first day until now" (Phil 1:3-5).

To the church of Thessalonica Paul wrote, "For what is our hope, or joy, or crown of rejoicing? Is it not even you in the presence of our Lord Jesus Christ at his coming? For you are our glory and joy" (1 Thes 2:19-20). When Luke referred to Paul's ministry to the Bereans, he wrote: "These were more fair-minded than those in Thessalonica, in that they received the word with all readiness, and searched the scriptures daily to find out whether these things were so" (Ac 17: 11). Paul must have anticipated with joy the matter of giving account of the churches in Philippi, Thessalonica, and Berea.

As churches heed the admonition of Scripture and follow the leadership of the pastor, they will encourage him and give him reason to anticipate the accounting day with joy.

In the final analysis, it is more often true that churches make great pastors than that pastors make great churches. May the undershepherds find such willing followship among their flocks that they may anticipate a joyful day of reckoning!

2. A Day of Reward

The pastor who has exemplified the Master, expounded the message of truth, and carefully examined his motives for ministry will one day be rewarded. Peter avowed, "When the Chief Shepherd appears, you will receive a crown of glory that does not fade away" (1 Pt 5:4).

At the judgment seat of Christ, five kinds of crowns will be given as rewards to the faithful servants of Jesus Christ. First there is the "incorruptible crown." Paul wrote the Corinthians, "Everyone who competes for the prize is temperate in all things. Now they do it to obtain a perishable crown; but we for an imperishable crown" (1 Cor 9:25). This is a reward for those who battle for Christ.

There is also a crown of rejoicing. In writing to the Philippian Christians, Paul referred to those whom he had won to Christ as his "joy and crown" (Phil 4:1). The crown of rejoicing is the soulwinner's crown (1 Thes 2: 20).

In his second letter to Timothy, Paul spoke of "the crown of righteousness" (2 Tm 4: 8). This crown is for those who have finished the race and who look forward to Christ's return and who will love His appearing. Faithful believers have the potential to receive this particular crown.

The Bible also speaks of "a crown of life." In the Lord's letter to the church of Smyrna, He declared, "Be faithful until death, and I will give you a crown of life" (Rv 2: 10). The worldly man lives to die, but the Christian man dies to live. Beyond this earthly existence for the child of God there is a new dimension of life more glorious than human comprehension can fathom.

The crown for the faithful pastor, however, is the crown of glory. The man of God who walked worthy of the vocation wherein he was called will hear the Lord's "well done thou good and faithful servant." His much-loved flock who helped him win the crown of glory by their submission to his leadership will also have the blessed privilege of sharing his reward. The Bible says, "He who receives a prophet in the name of a prophet shall receive a prophet's reward" (Mt 10:41).

As the faithful pastor and the beloved flock bow before the bema in humble gratitude for the receipt of the crown of glory the observant angels will shout a confirming "amen!"

Notes

1. https://standupforthetruth.com/2013/07/an-entertainment-driven-church/, accessed 02/25/2021

2. Elton Trueblood, *Your Other Vocation* (New York: Harper and Row Publishers, 1952), p. 53.

3. Chevis E. Horne, *Baptist Program*, April 1987.

4. https://www.challies.com/articles/why-i-am-not-egalitarian/, accessed 02/25/2021.

5. *Sistercelebration: Nine Worship Experiences* (Philadelphia: Fortress Press, 1974, pp.41-42).

6. John MacArthur, Jr., *Hebrews, The MacArthur New Testament Commentary* (Chicago: Moody Press, 1983), p. 445.

7. Daniel D. Walker, *Enemy in the Pew* (New York: Harper and Row Publishers, 1967), p. 183.

8. Ibid., p. 190.

CPSIA information can be obtained
at www.ICGtesting.com
Printed in the USA
FSHW021322040521